# Books That Changed Our Minds

# Books That Changed Our Minds

EDITED BY
MALCOLM COWLEY
& BERNARD SMITH

NEW YORK / THE KELMSCOTT EDITIONS

TO
# CHARLES A. BEARD
*—who teaches, writes and helps to make
the history of our times*

*Thanks are due to the editorial staff of
The New Republic, especially to* BRUCE
BLIVEN *and* GEORGE SOULE, *for their help
in this volume.*

*The biographical notes at the head of
each chapter were written by* BERNARD
SMITH, *using standard reference materials.*

# Contents

# Contents

# A Foreword on the Books That Changed Our Minds

Some readers will object that our minds are not changed by books, but rather by life itself, by what we do and suffer, by the world as observed with our own eyes and as reflected in our morning newspapers. What we get from books, they will say, is merely a confirmation and clarification of the ideas for which our experience had prepared us. Other readers will object that our minds are changed by the general current of opinion, as it reaches us in arguments and anecdotes, in magazine articles, plays and movies, radio talks, a dozen mediums of communication, some of them as formal as a university lecture series, others as casual and almost imperceptible as the new tone in a friend's voice when he speaks of a subject close to his heart. Books, they will say, are only one of these mediums, and not the most important.

There is truth in both these objections, which might lead to an interesting and practically endless discussion. It need not detain us here. For the present it is enough to say that sooner or later the life of our time is summarized in its books. Our new ideas are expressed there, whatever may be their original sources or the first mediums through which they reached us. It is books that form the permanent record, and books that furnish the most convenient basis for describing the mind of the world in which we live. In many ways it is a different mind from that of the world in which our fathers lived, and books at the very least have contributed to the change.

But which are the books that have contributed more than the others? That was the hardest problem we had to solve in planning this volume.

In the beginning it was Bernard Smith's idea. He suggested to the editors of The New Republic that they print a series of articles by different authors, each a specialist in his own field, revaluing the non-fiction works of the twentieth century that have contributed something new to American thinking. All the editors agreed with him that the idea was excellent. No two of them could agree with each other on the books that should be revalued. The arguments continued for several months, during which there were meetings with possible collaborators to discuss the project. These produced some sweeping judgments, some brilliant incidental remarks, a certain clarification of purpose, but no list of books that had changed our minds.

At this juncture we wrote to a number of friends for advice and personal comments. After describing the project and the difficulties involved in it, we asked, "What are the books in this category that have really impressed you and in some measure changed the direction of your thinking? So far the titles most frequently mentioned have been 'The Education of Henry Adams,' 'The Theory of the Leisure Class,' 'An Economic Interpretation of the Constitution,' 'Experience and Nature,' 'Main Currents in American Thought,' 'The Significance of Sections in American History'— and among the European books, Sorel's 'Reflections on Violence,' Croce's 'Esthetics,' Spengler's 'Decline of the West,' Freud's 'Interpretation of Dreams,' Pareto's 'Mind and Society' and perhaps some of the books by the 'new' scientists. But what are your suggestions?" The answers to this question would at least give us definite information on which to proceed.

## II

Everybody was interested in the problem; that was one thing the answers showed. In some cases the writer confined himself to the books—and the magazines, an interesting point—that had changed his own thinking; what he wrote was a brief intellectual biography. In other cases the writer mentioned books that seemed to have influenced people around him, his students or colleagues; what he wrote was a contribution to the general American background. But whether speaking subjectively or objectively, none of our correspondents fell into the common error of people who draw up lists of the "hundred best." That is, nobody pretended to have been impressed by books he thought other people would think he should have been impressed by, if he were the sort of person he thought they would think he ought to be.

Said Carl Becker, the historian, of Cornell University: "I have a letter from The New Republic which asks me to note any books during the last thirty or forty years which have impressed me or influenced my thinking. Undoubtedly many books have influenced my thinking, or at least clarified ideas I already had (which is about the only way books influence thinking anyway). Those I can think of offhand are the following:

"Sumner's 'Folkways,' which impressed me with the relativity of custom and ideas. Freud's 'Introduction to Psychoanalysis,' which made explicit the notion that the wish is father to the thought. Vaihinger's 'Als Ob,' which came to me in the English translation, 'As If,' and confirmed me in the notion that social thinking is shaped by certain unexamined preconceptions current at the time. Whitehead's 'Science and the Modern World' and 'Adventures of Ideas' had the same sort of influence. Croce's 'History, Its Theory and Practice' helped to shape my ideas about history, which I set forth in the address, 'Everyman His Own Historian.'

"What little I know about the new science has come largely through the popular works of Eddington, Whitehead and Bertrand Russell. (The latter's books on social matters are amusing but superficial.) Whitehead's little volume on mathematics in the Home University Library I found very useful. John Dewey's books I find hard to understand, but his ideas, coming to me through other writers, have confirmed a native tendency to pragmatic theory. Warner Fite's 'Moral Philosophy' is, I think, the only book on that subject that ever made any impression on me, but that hit the right spot somehow.

"I hope this may in some sense answer the request as you wish it to be answered."

Said Lewis Mumford, who later contributed the chapter on "The Decline of the West": "Your notion for a series of revaluations is excellent, and it ought to work out well. In addition to some of the books you mention I should add—with a sense that I have probably forgotten at the moment two or three of the most important books—the following:

> Whitehead: Science and the Modern World
> Sombart: Moderne Kapitalismus
> Bergson: Creative Evolution
> Kropotkin: Fields, Factories and Workshops
> Howard: The Garden City
> Branford: Science and Society
> Geddes and Thomson: Life

"The last volume is the only single book in which the major part of Geddes's ideas can be found. I should be tempted to substitute Brooks's 'America's Coming-of-Age' for Parrington. I hope you do a series on fiction too."

He added a postscript concerning an area of modern thinking that would be somewhat neglected by the other correspondents. "None of the books on your present list recognizes the important *biologizing* of thought that's going on—except possibly Spengler."

Said Assistant Attorney-General Thurman Arnold, then a professor in the Yale Law School: "I am not a particularly good person to consult on new contributions of ideas because I do not read good books. I am chiefly interested in editorials, judicial decisions, The Saturday Evening Post, the movies, speeches by university professors, The New Republic, The Nation—in fact, that stream of current literature which I am trying to analyze to get attitudes of the time. I read them and clip them to the exclusion of almost everything else. Of the titles you mention, I have read only 'The Education of Henry Adams' and 'The Economic Interpretation of the Constitution.' Pareto seemed to me an elaboration of the obvious, so I dropped it after a very cursory examination. Freud's contributions I have gotten entirely second hand.

"Therefore, my own notion of influential books is based on my guess as to what books have seeped down into popular consciousness. In other words, what literary ideas can you find reflected in the mine run of economic, scholarly and legal literature? My own guess would be that Freud's notion has been the most influential single thing. Second, Beard's 'Economic Interpretation of the Constitution,' also among the books you mention. If the others have had any influence at all, I am unable to see it, and I have been reading current stuff for years with the specific idea in mind of analyzing attitudes.

"Among the books you do not mention, I would say that Sinclair Lewis's 'Main Street' and 'Babbitt,' H. L. Mencken's criticism of the Rotarians, also George Bernard Shaw's somewhat objective attitude, Thorstein Veblen's analysis of American business, can all be traced. I do not know what books or plays of Shaw's or what particular writings of the others I would put first, but you can see all of them there.

"I would also add among influential writing The New Republic and The Nation. I have lived in three sections of the country: the Far West, West Virginia and Connecticut, and I have read The Nation and The New Republic consistently during all these years. I can tell what my liberal colleagues are going to say tomorrow by reading articles in these two publications today. In this country, periodical literature has been more important than books and there have been more new notions put across by these two publications than any other two in the history of American letters. I forgot Stuart Chase. Certainly there is no small town in the country where someone is not caught by his effective illustrations.

"However, I am violating the rules. What you wanted was books. If you have to select single books rather than writers, I am left with only two: first, Freud's 'Interpretation of Dreams' and second, Beard's 'Economic Interpretation of the Constitution.' No *single* book of Mencken, Chase or Sinclair Lewis can be listed on a par with these two. I am surprised at the selection of 'The Education of Henry Adams.' It is a great book, but it is a study in futility and I do not think has had any influence at all in an active, Rotarian and rip-snorting country like ours."

John Chamberlain, who was to write the chapter on "Folkways," had seven books to mention:

> Waldo Frank: Our America
> Van Wyck Brooks: America's Coming-of-Age
> Randolph Bourne: Untimely Papers
> Robert M. La Follette's Autobiography
> Theodore Dreiser: A Book About Myself
> William Graham Sumner: Folkways
> Alfred North Whitehead: Science and the Modern World

"I got jolts from these, primarily," he added. "Veblen and Beard were secondary influences. P.S. Not a Trotsky pamphlet on the list."

Kenneth Burke, the author of "Attitudes Toward History," discussed the same subject as Thurman Arnold, but from the standpoint of belles lettres rather than politics. "Your question," he said, "led me to wonder how much is done by individual, outstanding books, and how much by a general body of thought. Not some one work that jolts, but a steady pressure, supplied largely by periodicals. In my case, Smart Set, The Little Review, The Egoist, The Seven Arts and The Dial—all exemplifying, in one way or another, a general code that could be called the 'Esthetic Opposition' to the norms of business. Behind this, a mixture of psychoanalysis and economics, the interweaving of individual and social psychology one got in Bourne, Brooks, Frank. Now, looking back, it seems that the emphasis was largely *sociological,* even during those years when the talk of 'pure' form was at its height.

"Remy de Gourmont, who had a way of always seeming to say pleasant things, even when he was saying catastrophic ones. His fertile suggestions about the 'dissociation of ideas.' The essayistic novels of Huysmans, so much more essayistic than novelistic that they could legitimately be included here. They led into decadent Latin, of both pagan and evangelical sorts (and thence into a similar transition from Baudelaire to Rimbaud).

"I should hate to say so; but perhaps the biggest jolt I got from a single book in all this period was from Spengler's 'Untergang des Abendlandes,' which I read somewhere about 1920 (later making a translation of the ponderous and imposing introduction for The Dial). I believe that I have been trying to settle my score with this book ever since.

"This bogeyman should be dissipated, I think, by a mixture of Marxism and Ogden's Library of Philosophy, Psychology and Scientific Method. Here again was a body of thought, rather than a single work, that strongly affected me; though I should make exception of Ogden and Richards's 'Meaning of Meaning' and Richards's 'Principles of Literary Criticism.' The whole, however, is a desert-island collection. That is, I should think of it when answering the questionnaire that runs, 'If you were exiled to an isolated island, and all you could take with you were . . .' There would be 'Shakespeare, the Bible and the dictionary'—and then I'd begin thinking of Ogden's library.

"Add, for the next phase, the Encyclopedia of the Social Sciences. At least if one happens to believe that the most relevant thought of the twentieth century will be expended upon attempts at reintegration, and that sociology will assume in this work the role once assumed by metaphysics. But here again, of course, I'll be cheating, by offering a body of thought rather than any single monumental work."

Mr. Justice Frankfurter, then teaching at the Harvard Law School, sent a very short list: Croly's "Promise of American Life," Brandeis's "Other People's Money," Whitehead's "Science and the Modern World," Justice Holmes's "Collected Legal Papers." He added, "A grand idea."

Harold Laski, the political scientist, was the only Englishman to whom we wrote. "Of the books you mention," he said, "the only two that really impressed me were those of Beard and Parrington. They opened

windows for me into the significance of the American
tradition as no other books since Tocqueville. Of the
others, I was stimulated by Dewey and Freud, but not,
I think, in the sense of obtaining new and essential insights as I did from Beard and Parrington. Pareto
seemed to me the work of a superior sciolist; and I
have never understood the vogue of Henry Adams's
book; it is not in the class of Joseph Freeman's autobiography as an index to the essential America. I
should add to your list Lancelot Hogben's remarkable
book on mathematics."

Granville Hicks, the author of "The Great Tradition," discussed the list title by title. "I agree," he said,
"that 'The Education of Henry Adams,' 'The Theory
of the Leisure Class,' 'An Economic Interpretation of
the Constitution,' 'Main Currents' and 'The Significance of Sections' belong on the list. Although something of Dewey's ought to be included, I question 'Experience and Nature.' It seems to me that he made his
impact with 'Human Nature and Conduct.'

"The first of the American books that I would add
is 'The Autobiography of Lincoln Steffens.' Perhaps it
is felt that this is too recent. Nevertheless, I believe its
influence is not only very real but also possible to
estimate. The 'Autobiography' was almost the key
book of the depression. I have seen some of the thousands of letters that readers wrote to Steffens, and I
have myself talked with several score of college students who felt the book had done something to them.
Like Henry Adams, Steffens gave people not so much
new ideas as a new orientation, but even more than
Adams's, his book came at exactly the right moment.

"Surely you must have considered Croly's 'Promise of American Life,' Robinson's 'Mind in the Making,' and Babbitt's 'Rousseau and Romanticism.' None of these books, with the possible exception of Robinson's, had much influence on me, but a case could be made for them. A case could also be made for William James's 'Pragmatism,' Reed's 'Ten Days That Shook the World' and Krutch's 'The Modern Temper' (very influential in the colleges). And Bernard Smith and I agreed that it would be almost criminal to omit Woodrow Wilson—probably a more potent force on our generation than any other one person. Either 'The New Freedom' or his 'Collected Speeches' could be considered.

"Among the European books, Croce, Spengler and Freud seem to me absolutely necessary. Sorel, as an influence on American thought, is not quite so clear, and I am very dubious indeed about Pareto. Has he as yet had any real influence over here?

"It does seem to me that Lenin ought to be included, probably 'Imperialism.' You can't very well include 'Capital,' but you can include the book that most of us read before we read 'Capital.' It is true that Marxist influence has come through many books, not through one, but it ought not be ignored for that reason.

"I might add that a very real influence on me was Shaw, though I can't point to any one book."

Paul Weiss, of the faculty at Bryn Mawr, wrote from the standpoint of the technical philosopher. "All the books on your list seem to me important, with the possible exception of Pareto's. This looks to me to be a purely literary choice, to which you could get very few sociologists, economists or philosophers to subscribe. Grant, against the evidence, that it is a good book; whose thinking has it modified? I have some doubts about 'The Education of Henry Adams' and the 'Main Currents,' though I cannot really qualify as a judge. And I doubt very much whether you have chosen the right book of Dewey. 'Experience and Nature' is his most important technical work, but so difficult and sluggish that I suspect that it has had very little influence. Dewey ought of course to be included, but I think you ought to choose his writings on education if you want him at his most influential, or perhaps his 'Human Nature and Conduct.' Your list seems to be overloaded on the economic-historical side and I am afraid emphasizes those books which have been most influential with or most discussed by literary rather than technical or speculative thinkers.

"Subject to recall without notice, here are my ten:

Veblen's Theory of the Leisure Class
James's Pragmatism
Dewey's Human Nature and Conduct (?)
Watson's Behaviorism
Freud's Interpretation of Dreams
Einstein's Relativity
Russell's Knowledge of the External World
Whitehead's Science and the Modern World
Spengler's Decline of the West
The Gestalt School—Wertheimer, Köhler, Koffka

"I think very little of some of these, but I have no doubt of their great influence in many domains. A list of the *best* books would be different."

Newton Arvin, who teaches American Literature at Smith, sent a list of twenty books that included "The

Principles of Literary Criticism," by I. A. Richards,
"The Life of Reason," by George Santayana, "The
Great Society," by Graham Wallas, "Our America,"
by Waldo Frank, "The Mind in the Making," by
James Harvey Robinson and the Epistle Dedicatory to
"Man and Superman." "There is," Arvin said, explaining his standard of choice, "a difference between the
particular books one realizes have actually impressed
oneself and made a difference in one's thinking at some
(perhaps very youthful) period, and the books that
one can see have deservedly had a great and general
influence. For example, I shouldn't feel like claiming
anything of the sort for 'Our America' or 'The Mind
in the Making,' though they affected me very much
fifteen years ago or so. Also, I have not listed again
any of the books that you have specified, though I
should myself have to acknowledge the effect of Parrington and Veblen: not so much of Henry Adams
(who has always repelled me), and not at all of Croce
(whom I never read or very much cared to) or Spengler (whom I was perhaps too lazy to read but felt a
strong distaste for at second hand).

"I am startled, in a way, to see how few French or
German books I have read of this sort—books written
in the last thirty or forty years, I mean. If one could
go back to the eighteenth or nineteenth century, it
would be a very different matter; but that is not the
point. I hardly know what French or German writers
*could* have had a great effect on us except for certain
novelists or playwrights. I imagine that for Frenchmen
and Germans there are plenty of writers to correspond
to Wallas and Russell and Santayana and Beard—how

few of whom, in either case, have very much authority outside their own language and parish.

"I have read, too, something of Jeans and Eddington, but either not very understandingly or not very sympathetically. These idealistic physicists seem to me pretty much to be Baptists or Quakers disguised behind telescopes or mortar-boards. Wells's and Huxley's book, 'The Science of Life,' which I suppose has never had any currency with literary sophisticates (and is in any case not a great original contribution to thought), strikes me as much more provocative imaginatively and, in a secondary way, much more truly in the great main current of modern thought."

Said Clifton Fadiman, the literary critic of The New Yorker: "An interesting question. Probably none of the answers, including this one, will be honest. No one remembers what books really impressed one, or changed the direction of one's thought. Two forbidden pages out of some tawdry 'sex book,' read when one was eleven, may have had more influence on one than all the works by Freud. Also, one isn't influenced so much by specific books as by streams of tendency, popularized notions, rehashes of ideas. I suppose our generation has been more influenced by Marx than by any other single writer—yet very few of us, certainly not myself, have really read much Marx. Still, if you must have a list, here is mine:

Spengler's Decline of the West
The Prefaces and Plays of George Bernard Shaw
The early books of Van Wyck Brooks
V. I. Lenin's Imperialism
Freud generally

John Strachey's The Coming Struggle for Power
P. W. Bridgman's The Logic of Modern Physics
Sir Arthur Eddington's The Nature of the Physical World
The early books by H. L. Mencken
In a general way, all the biographies of scientists that I
    happen to have read in the last fifteen years—such a one
    as Vallery-Radot's Pasteur, for example.

Said I. F. Stone, then writing editorials for The Nation and The New York Post: "The book that first got
me started was Jack London's 'Martin Eden.' In its
pages I obtained my first glimpse of the modern world
of thought (I was twelve at the time) and because of
it I read Herbert Spencer's 'First Principles' and
learned about Darwinism. The next big step I remember
was when at fourteen in a summer hotel I first discovered The New Republic and The Nation, back numbers of which were under the parlor table. Next poetry:
first Carl Sandburg, then Milton's 'Paradise Lost,' and
'Samson Agonistes,' then a Mermaid edition of Mar-
lowe, *usw.*

"Aside from Emerson and Thoreau, whom I discovered early and loved, the first American work of
non-fiction that I can remember as really marking a
step forward in my intellectual development was
Beard's 'Economic Interpretation of the Constitution,'
which I discovered in the Camden Public Library while
I was a reporter on the old Courier. I was already,
roughly speaking at least, a Marxist by that time (the
eye-opener here was Kropotkin's 'Conquest of Bread,'
whence I went on to Marx, Bukharin's 'Historical Materialism' and Engels) but this book made me realize
the possibilities of American history and sociology.
Louis Boudin's 'Government by Judiciary' was also an

eye-opener for me, although I had already obtained a
fair glimpse of the subject before I read it."

Robert S. Lynd, the author of "Middletown" and
"Middletown in Transition," did not write this sort of
intellectual autobiography, but he sent a list of reading
that serves the same purpose. "Instead of giving you a
general evaluation," he said, "I'd rather try to name
the books that have put the peculiar English on this
particular billiard ball. Princeton was an intellectual
vacuum for me so far as non-literary books go. I had
to wait until I got out to come alive to all my present
interests. Here are the things that stand out as I have
fumbled about since 1914:

> J. A. Hobson: Work and Wealth
> Felix Adler: An Ethical Philosophy of Life
> John Dewey: Essays in Experimental Logic; Reconstruc-
> tion in Philosophy; Human Nature and Conduct; and
> his long opening essay in the group volume on Creative
> Intelligence
> Veblen: Theory of Business Enterprise; Engineers and the
> Price System; Absentee Ownership; The Place of
> Science; The Theory of the Leisure Class
> William James: Letters
> T. H. Huxley: Letters
> Clark Wissler: Man and Culture
> A. R. Brown: The Andaman Islanders (Chapter V)
> Samuel Butler: Erewhon
> R. H. Tawney: Religion and the Rise of Capitalism
> J. L. and Barbara Hammond: The Town Laborer (Chap-
> ters X–XV)
> Lewis Corey: The Decline of American Capitalism
> Papers by Wesley Mitchell in various journals (later col-
> lected in his Backward Art of Spending Money)
> Papers by Lawrence K. Frank: e.g., The Management of
> Tensions, in the American Journal of Sociology for

March, 1928; The Development of Science, in the Journal of Philosophy, January, 1924."

There were other letters, and good ones too. Louis Hacker, the historian, sent a valuable list, including several books that others had completely neglected— Myers's "History of the Great American Fortunes," Mathiez's "The French Revolution," Zimmern's "The Greek Commonwealth," Trotsky's "History of the Russian Revolution" and a work I thought that everyone would mention, Sir James G. Frazer's "The Golden Bough." . . . Said Charles A. Beard, "Brooks Adams's two books are thumping." I think he was referring to "The Law of Civilization and Decay" and "Theory of Social Revolutions." He continued, "Mannheim's 'Ideology and Utopia' should certainly be included, and Croce's 'History, Its Theory and Practice.'" . . . Lionel Trilling, the critic, wanted us to discuss "The Sacred Wood" and "Mont-Saint-Michel and Chartres." . . . Bernard Smith put in a strong plea for Pavlov's "Lectures on Conditioned Reflexes." . . . Leo Huberman, the author of "We, the People," listed a dozen learned titles, then added a postscript: "Of course the books that influenced me most, certainly as a young child, were Horatio Alger's."

In the letters taken as a whole, the titles that recurred most frequently were "An Economic Interpretation of the Constitution" and "The Theory of the Leisure Class"; each of these received eight mentions. "The Decline of the West" received seven, "The Interpretation of Dreams" received six, and five mentions each were received by "The Education of Henry Adams," "Human Nature and Conduct," "Main Currents in American Thought," the Prefaces of George Bernard

Shaw, "Science and the Modern World" and "The Theory of Business Enterprise." Counting authors instead of titles, Thorstein Veblen came first with sixteen mentions. Next came Charles A. Beard (eleven), John Dewey (ten), Sigmund Freud (nine), Oswald Spengler and Alfred North Whitehead (seven each), V. I. Lenin (six) and I. A. Richards (six, including his collaboration with C. K. Ogden). There were a few surprising omissions, including Wells's "Outline of History," the most popular non-fiction work of the 1920's. Einstein got only two votes; Havelock Ellis and Bergson got one apiece. For the most part it seems to be American books that have influenced the American mind.

### III

These letters were obviously not to be taken as a Gallup poll of American reading habits. On that subject, Dr. Gallup has taken his own poll. Through the Institute of Public Opinion, he asked Americans "in all parts of the country and in all walks of life" to name the most interesting book they had ever read. Out of the twenty books most frequently mentioned in 1938, there were eighteen novels, and almost all of these were novels that had been made into popular motion pictures. The two non-fiction works were the Bible, standing first in the list, and "How to Win Friends and Influence People," standing fifth. In the northeastern states, the Bible was mentioned less often than "Gone with the Wind." Dr. Gallup's poll agrees in a general way with the report made by Robert S. Lynd in Chapter XVII of "Middletown," and again in Chapter VII of "Middletown in Transition." Of the books taken from the Middletown public library in 1935, only 15.8 percent were non-fiction. The books that Middletown read and liked were completely different from the books that Mr. Lynd mentioned in his letter as having "put the peculiar English on this particular billiard ball."

But although our letters were written by men belonging to a very small sector of the American public, with special training and special interests, still they were not without value as evidence. Our correspondents were educators, historians, critics, lecturers or publicists—in other words, they were men directly or indirectly engaged in the business of molding the public mind. When they listed the books that had affected their own ideas, they were also discussing, by implication, the ideas they are passing on to their students or their readers. Few of the books they mentioned have been popular; not one has been a best-seller in this country; but most of them are reaching the public at second hand.

With these letters in front of us, our problem of choosing a dozen books for revaluation was vastly simplified. We did not propose to follow the suggestions mechanically, in the sense of merely counting mentions. On the other hand, we had learned that certain books, or rather certain authors like Veblen, Beard, Dewey, Freud and Spengler, would have to be included. Other authors whom we had thought of treating were eliminated by the fact that they met with a negative response, like Pareto, or with almost no response at all, like Bergson and Sorel. About half our list was still in doubt. Before deciding on it, we should have to consider new factors—for example the desirability of choosing different types of books representing the different trends in modern thought, and the difficulty of finding men qualified to deal with two or three authors we thought of including. There were still more debates before we agreed on our twelve titles.

And even these were not a final list. This book from beginning to end has been a collaboration, and the men who wrote the separate chapters also helped to decide the subjects. Often they argued for one book as against another, and won the argument, as specialists. Thus, the most frequently mentioned book by John Dewey was "Human Nature and Conduct," but when the chapter came to be written, C. E. Ayres decided that Dewey's contribution to logic had been fundamental, and accordingly centered the discussion around "Studies in Logical Theory." In the same way Lenin's "Imperialism," with four mentions, gave way to "The State and Revolution," with only two. The contributors each wrote for himself. Sometimes they disagreed with the editors or with one another, as compare what George Soule says about psychoanalysis with what Paul Radin implies about it in his chapter on "The Mind of Primitive Man." Yet the book as a whole expresses a unified point of view, which is that of liberalism in our own century.

Even from this one point of view, it would be impossible to choose the twelve or the twenty books that have most deeply influenced modern American thinking. Our final list, as it appears in the table of contents, involves a whole series of compromises, and more than one arbitrary choice disguised as an editorial judgment. It is easy to criticize for what it omits, since the American mind has many more facets than are revealed in the books under discussion. On that subject I shall have more to say in a final chapter. But the list is harder to criticize for what it includes, since each of these twelve books has exerted a real influence in its own field of thought and now deserves a careful re-valuation. Most of them not only have changed but are continuing to change our minds.

M. C.

# I.

# Freud and "The Interpretation of Dreams"

By GEORGE SOULE

SIGMUND FREUD was born on May 6, 1856, at Freiberg, Moravia, which was formerly part of the Czecho-Slovakian Republic. His parents were Jews—"and I have remained a Jew myself," he wrote. At the age of four he was taken to Vienna, where he grew up, was educated, and spent practically all of his adult life. He went to the University of Vienna to study medicine, receiving his M.D. in 1881. In 1882 he entered the General Hospital, where he continued his studies in neurology and cerebral anatomy. In 1885 he was awarded a Traveling Fellowship and went to Paris. It was a turning point of his life, for here he encountered Charcot's work on hysteria and his treatment of it by hypnotic suggestion.

Back in Vienna he began to study the case of a young girl observed by Dr. Joseph Breuer, in whose case he first discovered the element of sexuality as a factor in neurosis. He began to make similar investigations into the lives of his own patients. "Studies of Hysteria" was his first book in this field. "The Interpretation of Dreams," published in 1900, was scarcely reviewed by the technical journals and was derided in medical schools, but it slowly attracted imitators and disciples. In 1909 Freud was introduced to America through a series of lectures at Clark University.

After writing "Totem and Taboo," which he published in 1912, he was less concerned with psychoanalysis as a medical technique and more concerned with cultural problems, especially religion. When Hitler seized Austria in the spring of 1938, Freud's flight from Vienna to London was front-page news in the papers of all but the fascist countries. He remained in England until his death, on September 23, 1939. His most recent work, "Moses and Monotheism," was published in the summer of 1939. Other well known books of his, with dates of first publication in English, are "The Psychopathology of Everyday Life" (1914), "Beyond the Pleasure Principle" (1924), "The Ego and the Id" (1927) and "Introductory Lectures on Psychoanalysis" (1929).

THERE ARE intellectual discoverers whose influence is measured largely by a single postulate or theory—like Harvey with the circulation of the blood, Koch and Pasteur with the germ theory of disease, or even Newton with gravitation. But there are others who contribute not merely specific discoveries but a point of view that brings about subtle and far-reaching changes in the way people think. Of this nature was Darwin with his concept of evolution, Marx with his dynamic explanation of social change, and Freud with his view of the human personality. Regardless of the scientific testing of specific hypotheses, such illuminations furnish a general framework into which a large number of things seem to fit, a clue to hitherto unexplored regions, the sort of organic explanation of many relationships, which people see as a more consistent ordering of previous insights. These discoverers leave their traces in language, coining words and phrases that are accepted in common usage by many who have only vague ideas of the theories in which the terms originally played a part.

Innovators of this kind are likely to suffer a peculiar fate. Not only do they shock vested interests in doctrine and arouse bitter opposition but, because of the fundamental nature of their challenge, they frighten on an even wider front those who depend for security on established ideas and *mores*. Their influence often makes its way not so much by reasoned acceptance or rejection as by the permeation of disguised agents into the ranks of the opposition—agents in the form of ideas and methods that survive because they remain useful, even to those who reject the main body of theory from which they came. So, many an economist who today analyzes the contradictions of capitalism does not stop to think that these ideas stem from Marx, whose more formal constructions he vigorously rejects. And many who regard Freud as the originator of a mistaken theory would not know how to get along without the concept of unconscious motivation, or the word "complex," or the understanding of certain people's behavior in terms of father-fixation or dependence on maternal care.

Perhaps the most common error about Freud is to think of him as a philosopher who sat down in his study and wove out of his mind an intellectual system, which he set down in a book. Such books are the subject of debate, and eventually find their place in the catalogue of thought; they can be tested by the reason of anyone who reads them. People who regard Freud in this way—a way that is far more nearly true of Marx or even of Darwin—are likely to believe that when his work burst on the world some thirty years ago, it was accepted as a fad, gave us some useful hints and then retreated into its historical niche like a winter's fashion.

It is true that the new ideas he introduced were at the beginning exploited by a host of those who understood them imperfectly. Like many others, he suffered from too much popularization. The distortion of the cult wreaked its usual havoc. But Freud himself was never a system-maker or the leader of a popular movement. He was a practising physician, with a solid scientific background. The genius which gave him an extraordinary insight into the mysteries of personality was not exercised in intellectual divination or the arrangement of abstract ideas, but in dealing with individual patients in the doctor's office; what he discovered he learned from them, from the cures and failures that resulted from the treatment. Like any good scientist, he held preconceived ideas in check; as the laboratory worker looks through the microscope to see what he can find, so he looked by the various methods he devised into the minds and behavior of his patients. He has been engaged in a continual learning process; his earlier techniques and hypotheses have subsequently been modified or refined. The main body of his scientific contribution cannot be found in any single book or paper—even though such a work as "The Interpretation of Dreams" offers a suggestive introduction or his later "Autobiography" a lucid summary. And it cannot be evaluated simply by common-sense criticism. It is rather open to confirmation or rejection only by competent persons who have received the arduous professional training necessary to test it by experiment in the same kind of human laboratory that supplied him with his data. For the layman to argue about the validity of psychoanalytic therapy is as fruitless as for him to attempt a critical discussion of brain surgery.

Freud's first work to emphasize the distinction between the conscious mind and the unconscious was "Studies of Hysteria," published in 1895. Although the existence of the unconscious had previously been recognized, Freud was the first to explore it systematically and to develop a technique of therapy based upon it. "The Interpretation of Dreams" (1900) explained, with many examples, how he used dreams for this purpose. It set forth the theory that dreams are an expression of wish fulfillment, that they have latent and hidden meanings as well as those lying nearer the surface, and that they are distorted and condensed by the action of the censor. Implicit in this book also is the theory of the libido, with Freud's early views of the famous Oedipus complex. Later works added to and corrected these conceptions. Whereas at the beginning Freud thought it enough to trace the hidden springs of emotion in the libido, he later stressed the additional importance of the analysis of the ego and of the character.

Though the original popular interest in psychoanalytic theory has abated, its contributions to science have kept on quietly expanding through the work of the ever growing number of its trained practitioners, until it has become accepted as one of the established resources of medicine. Analysts are on the teaching staffs of some of the best medical schools. General psychiatry has made use of the Freudian contribution. Today, in the United States, the recognized psychoanalyst must have his degree in general medicine from an approved school; he must have gone through a general medical interneship, a special psychiatric interneship and the training requisite for a specialist in psychiatry; and, finally, he must have been analyzed himself, must learn his art under the direction of the local Psychoanalytic Institute, and must be approved by it. It should therefore be remembered that the nucleus of what we are discussing is not a book or a system of thought but a living and changing scientific discipline that is constantly at work in the practice of medicine. And, in this sphere at least, it must be recognized that Freud's influence has become more and more solidly established, even though, like other medical innovators, he still has to encounter opposition within the profession.

What does badly need to be done, however, is to evaluate and correct the influences that have flowed out from the nub of medical theory into literature, personal standards, general scientific and social thinking.

## II

Freud's theories, with their insights into unconscious motivation and emotional abnormalities, seemed at first to offer a large vein of new material to the creative writer, and were widely utilized both in subject matter and in method. Yet it is doubtful that their extensive influence resulted in any great enrichment of literature. The poet has his own insights into human personality, and he employed them according to his talents long before psychoanalysis was ever heard of. The literary creations best subject to psychoanalytic interpretation were written without reference to Freudian theory.

They are simply the poems, plays and novels that evince the most sensitive understanding of personality and emotion. And there is every reason why this should be so. The good psychoanalyst is himself something of a poet; he knows from experience that nothing is so deadening to the appreciation of a given individuality as the crude application of some general formula that may not fit the person in question. To approach a task of artistic evocation with the scaffolding of an intellectual theory often inhibits those very insights upon which the creative success of the writer depends. The best writers in the proletarian school, no less than in the Freudian, have discovered this truth. The function, both of the writer and of the psychiatrist, is not to fit every personality to a Procrustean bed of preconceived notions, but to observe, each in his own way and for his own purposes, what the personality is made of and how it behaves. Significant parallels are discovered only after the literary evidence is in.

The influence of psychoanalytic conceptions on style has been even more pervasive than their influence on matter or interpretation. There has been a marked tendency to the use of words, not as clearly denotative descriptions, but as symbols or as starting points for a long train of association enriched by the unconscious. Processes of "free association" have been practised in writing, with the idea of liberating language and getting away from trite and stereotyped images. This tendency has sometimes extended to a point of complete unintelligibility; in the case of some of the most highly praised writers, such as James Joyce or Gertrude Stein, exhaustive glossaries or interpretations are necessary before the average reader can make anything out of them. Painters and sculptors, too, have attempted to delve directly into the preconscious or even the unconscious by the use of unfamiliar symbols rather than by employing the customary methods of pictorial description. Not all the influence in these directions may be traced to Freud; there were many factors in the intellectual atmosphere that contributed to the new modes of art.

These styles are not likely to be widely imitated or to endure long. They have had their effect on others who develop in a less extreme fashion the hints provided; they have probably served a purpose in loosening, deformalizing and vivifying language. At the same time there is a reaction against them as a means of escape into "art for art's sake"—a mode of expression that has no connection with a popular audience or with social meanings. As such, they are as far as possible from the therapeutic aims of psychoanalysis itself, which investigates the unconscious, not to exploit it or to provide a way out from everyday existence, but precisely in order to neutralize its deceptions and make unnecessary false escapes from reality. Words as symbols carrying rich associations have been used by poets from time immemorial, without departure from meaning. It may be significant in this connection that Freud himself has an extraordinarily lucid and logical style; he does not even veil his meaning more than is unavoidable in the technical terms that scientists usually affect. The freedom from emotional blocks which he has achieved is devoted to releasing his rationality and persuasiveness rather than the reverse. The consequence of being a skilled psychiatrist is not to write like one of his patients.

Popular misunderstanding of psychoanalytic ideas had for a time an equally curious effect on personal conduct. Those who half understood it, from reading only, often assumed that it taught that the basis of life was untrammeled emotional impulse and that, in order to be healthy, it was necessary merely to banish every inhibition that might prevent one from doing whatever one felt like at the moment. Of course it is true that some patients suffer from repression of unconscious drives, which then manifest themselves in a deformed aspect through bodily illness or neurotic behavior, and that the task of the doctor is often to bring to consciousness the guilt or hate or fear that is troubling them in a disguised form.

But that is only half the battle; the patient then has to learn to behave like a complete and civilized being without denying the existence of his emotions—but also without expressing them in injurious or crazy ways. He has to get them in harness, using them instead of allowing them to drive him. This is an exercise in reason and character indeed. A person who is nothing but a bundle of raw and conflicting emotions is fit only for a madhouse or a prison. Freud's therapeutic technique is not to deny reason in the interest of instinctual life, but rather to strengthen reason by preventing it from being warped by unrecognized and, therefore, untamed and destructive emotion. He believes that the healthy individual must have freedom, to be sure—but not only freedom from stupid external restrictions that cramp life, but also freedom from irrational compulsions within himself. Such freedom implies organization and discipline.

The exaltation of the irrational in social or political life is likewise often unjustly attributed to the influence of Freud. His discovery of the enormous part played by the unconscious in the human mind—which is often compared to an iceberg, only one-seventh of which is seen above the surface of the water—is frequently thought to destroy the hope of rational progress, and to make necessary the treatment of human beings as if they were creatures that can be influenced only by emotional propaganda rather than by appeals to reason. It is sometimes supposed that the Fascists and the Nazis learned their cynical technique from this school of thought, or that indeed their pursuit of irrational goals is justified by the kind of animal man is. Religious moralists, particularly those of the Aristotelian or Thomist school, deplore what they believe is Freud's exaltation of the impulsive, and call for a return to reason and the acceptance of basic truths long since discovered and handed down by authority.

But in fact, if Freud's discovery is valid, the unconscious with its irrational influence was there long before he found it; he did not create it. Men were moved by emotion contrary to reason long before he was born, and Hitler and Mussolini are not the first anti-humanist leaders. The important question is whether Freud is correct, not whether one deplores the truth he found. Of course one can argue that if this sort of thing is so it is better not to know it, but one cannot argue that and still retain any respect for science or for reason itself. Indeed there lies a hope for reason in human affairs in the proper use of the discoveries Freud has made. If the unconscious *does* influence us powerfully

in irrational directions, then the more we explore it—
and thus make it less unconscious—the better able we
are to dissolve the destructive influences of its conflicts,
and gain power from its creative drives. Reason can
begin to be effective in purposeful transformation of
reality only when it begins to be freed from unconscious
biases. And it is the function of psychoanalysis to serve
just this end.

Resistance to the discovery that one is influenced by
unknown and disreputable emotions as well as by reason, morality and conscious will is a universal trait of
analytic patients—to admit that this is true seems like
an insult to the dignity of the ego. And the stronger the
irrational influence, the greater, as a rule, is the resistance to acknowledging that it exists, for that resistance
is the very thing that maintains the repression and
keeps the emotion unconscious. It is therefore no surprise that in philosophic discussion we should find
strong opposition to the idea of unconscious motivation; those who lay great stress on this point are themselves open to the suspicion of unconscious bias. It is
probable that their objections may be explained on
some other ground than that of pure reason. Few if
any of them have taken the pains conscientiously to
examine the facts that lead to acceptance of the theory;
they simply reject it because they disapprove of it. Centuries of authoritative "truth," however, have not bred
a race that a disinterested observer could call highly
rational.

Psychoanalytic ideas have been extended also to
biography, anthropology and history. The results have
been suggestive, but not definitive. It is natural to sup-

pose that whatever throws light on the behavior of known individuals will also illuminate the behavior of individuals in other places or generations, and even of groups, tribes and nations. This is undoubtedly true. Yet no good doctor makes a confident diagnosis of a patient whom he can actually see and study, without a careful examination; even then he may be wrong. Long-distance diagnosis is therefore perilous. And if we cannot be sure about the sources of behavior even of a single person concerning whom a good many facts are not recorded, how much less can we infer with any certainty what really determines the action of a group or society which, though as a whole it may conform to certain observed patterns, still consists of personalities as yet unexplored.

When psychoanalysts themselves write concerning subjects outside their own practice, it is not always clear just when they depart from scientific assurance and advance mere guesses or hypotheses. This confuses the reader, and makes him suspect that the ability of psychoanalysis to throw light on non-medical subjects has been overemphasized. It should be accepted as a premise that psychological work in these non-medical fields is still in a pioneer stage, and what is written about it must necessarily be tentative. Once that warning is laid down, however, there can be no doubt that modern psychology has much to offer; indeed the social disciplines could hardly make further progress without it. The moment they branch out from pure description to any sort of theoretical formulation, they necessarily make assumptions about human character and motivation. The psychological assumptions that are likely to be accepted by one who knows nothing about the structure of the personality beyond the uncritical ideas of the layman are likely to be inferior to those of one who is professionally familiar with the mind.

In this respect the common objection that the doctors deal only with abnormalities does not carry much weight. There is no sharp dividing line between the normal and the abnormal, but rather a continuous gradation, and it is impossible to understand either without knowing a good deal about the other. To say that a psychiatrist is incapable of accounting for healthy behavior because his function is curing the sick is like saying that a physician who deals primarily with bodily illness therefore cannot understand the ordinary facts of anatomy and the processes of physiology.

### III

Perhaps the greatest resistance to understanding of psychoanalysis comes, not from the moralists, but from the tradition of thought which is crudely materialistic and insists on tracing every phenomenon to a purely physical cause. By those accustomed to think in this way, it is supposed that Freud set out to deal with the "psyche" as opposed to the body and that hence there must be an element of unscientific mysticism in his method. Pavlov, as a physiologist, is approved because he modified animal behavior by external conditioning, whereas Freud is regarded distrustfully because his treatment consists so largely of examining and rearranging ideas and emotions. Yet many of Freud's cases— including early ones—were people who were obviously physically ill. The better scientific theory of today regards as false the theoretical separation between material and mental. The human body is a living organism which is in itself neither wholly physical nor wholly mental, but both. Its behavior has both aspects at once; the reality behind them is unitary. The discipline of the psychiatrist and that of the physiologist are not separate divisions of subject matter; they are merely different avenues by which identical phenomena may be approached.

It is clear, for instance, that Freud's theories about character formation in the child depend, not merely on his discoveries of the way in which the mind works, but on the kind of conditioning that the child receives from his environment—a conditioning which is no less and no more physical than the environments which Pavlov created for his dogs. The "conditioned reflex" fits perfectly into psychoanalytic theory, for without it there would be no understanding of the behavior trait by which persons early habituated to respond in a certain way to certain stimuli often continue to do so after any rational cause for the response is gone. And this trait is at the very bottom of many neuroses.

Psychiatric treatment has sometimes been most successful in cases of what has customarily been regarded as purely physical disease—for instance, heart trouble, digestive disturbances, allergies and skin lesions. This is true, not merely when the ailment in question is hysterical or, as the layman says, "imaginary," but when its symptoms are established by the most rigorous physical tests. On the other hand, physical therapy, such as insulin or metrazol shock, is having amazing success in relieving the symptoms of what used to be regarded as purely mental disease, such as schizophrenia—a disorder that resists psychoanalysis when far advanced. The result of such recent discoveries is the establishment of a new frontier of medicine in which the psychiatrist and the other medical specialists are beginning to work together both in research and in therapy. The good psychiatrist is always alert for physical symptoms in what used to be called "mental" disease, while the other medical specialists are gradually learning that many, if not most, "physical" diseases have important emotional components, and that it is the whole patient that must be treated rather than just the symptom.

A similar unnecessary opposition has existed in social thinking. It has been supposed by some that psychoanalysis deals entirely with the individual and attributes all the ills of the world to personal abnormalities and mistakes, whereas social difficulties really arise mainly from environmental causes and can be remedied only by social or political action. The psychoanalyst, it is thought, believes simply in adjusting the individual to his environment, whereas the greater necessity is to adjust the environment to individuals. It is true, of course, that the doctor's main business is treating single patients, and since it is impossible for him to remake the whole social order overnight, a large part of his task must be assisting the individual to achieve greater health within civilization as it exists. But it is not true that psychoanalytic theory leads to the conclusion that social change is undesirable or that anyone who believes in it is abnormal. Indeed, some of the most abnormal persons are the stubbornly conservative. It is a sign of neurotic character to be unwilling to change an environment when it is reasonable to do so for purposes of survival or health.

Much of the psychiatrist's repair work might be

avoided in a social order that was modified in respect of
family institutions, education and organization of adult
life; it ought to be possible to derive from psychiatric
knowledge extremely valuable conclusions concerning
the kind of modifications that should be made, as well
as techniques for achieving them. Just as individuals
would be inconceivable without external relationships,
so social problems cannot really be understood without
accurate knowledge of the way in which individuals
behave in relation to each other and to groups. To
conceive of watertight compartments between the individual and society is as erroneous as to separate in a
similar manner the body and the mind. The real distinction lies not so much in the subject matter as in the
angle of approach. Cross-fertilization between the two
ways of studying human behavior—the psychological
and the social—is still in its infancy, but we already
know enough to suspect that here lies the next great
hope for the advancement of science in the study of
mankind.

# II.

# "The Education of Henry Adams"

## By LOUIS KRONENBERGER

HENRY ADAMS was born in Boston on February 16, 1838. He was the third son of Charles Francis Adams, who was United States minister to England during the Civil War. His grandfather was John Quincy Adams, sixth President of the United States, and his great-grandfather was John Adams, the second President. His brothers became eminent lawyers and men of affairs.

He went to Harvard College, from which he was graduated in 1858. Then followed a year of study in Berlin and a year of travel through Germany and Italy. He returned to the United States in 1860 and became secretary to his father, who was then a congressman. In the same capacity he accompanied his father to London, where he remained until 1868. For two years thereafter he was in Washington observing the political scene and contributing articles to The North American Review, The Nation, and The New York Evening Post. In 1870 he became an assistant professor of History at Harvard and editor of The North American Review, but after seven years he retired from both posts to devote himself entirely to writing.

In 1879 he published his first book, "The Life of Albert Gallatin," and in 1880 his anonymous novel, "Democracy." At the same time he was working on his "History of the United States of America during the Administrations of Thomas Jefferson and James Madison," which was published serially, in nine volumes, 1889–91. "Mont-Saint-Michel and Chartres" was privately printed in an edition of 150 copies in 1904; 100 copies of "The Education of Henry Adams" were printed in 1906 and distributed to his friends. These are the two books in which Adams tried to express his personal philosophy. The first was revised in 1911 and reissued for the public in 1913. Adams also intended to revise the second, with which he was never satisfied, but a paralytic stroke in 1912 made further literary work impossible. The "Education" did not appear in a trade edition until six months after his death in 1918.

FOUR GENERATIONS after one member of the Adams family helped compose the Declaration of Independence, another sat down and wrote a book declaring it null and void. So rapidly had events come to pass that it required just a century and a quarter to demolish America's greatest act of faith with her most withering words of denial. Between John Adams and his great-grandson Henry lay the total wreck of a dream. The disaster had robbed Henry Adams not only of his illusions but equally of his usefulness; the thing that had come about was beyond Henry Adams's ability to cope with or fight against or repair; he, who had burned to participate in American life, was reduced to becoming its stern and dissident historian. Hence, to confess his own failure, and to reveal the far greater failure that had brought his own about, and to fail (as he thought) in confessing it, Adams sat down and wrote the "Education."

The "Education" found its most responsive readers

in those years following the World War when they too
had reason to believe that American life had failed
them; and to every American intellectual who still retained inside him vestiges of the American moralist,
Adams's grim citation of a century's crimes and blunders helped explain the plight of the modern world.
The demonstration seemed Euclidean enough to justify the bitterly ironic tone which overhung it: for here
was Henry Adams, supremely well born, talented,
eager, thoughtful, industrious, confessing that every
ideal he owned had been traduced; insisting that the
world of action had been impossible to enter, and the
world of thought powerless to give hope. Only chaos,
explosion, cataclysm loomed ahead. A sensitive person
was better out of life; in it, a Henry Adams could only
by turns shudder and grow brutally cynical.

The book which reached these conclusions remains
an important document of American intellectual and
moral inquiry, if only because not a dozen Americans
of any period were intellectually and morally of a stat-
ure to produce it. It is predicated of very nearly a first-
rate mind and something like a first-rate experience. If
the mind fails us, it is chiefly from not being purposeful enough; if the experience, it is from being largely
of one kind. Adams came to know everything within
the reach of the cultivated man of the world, everything to be had of drawing-rooms and libraries, colleges
and clubs, churches and ruins, senates and courts; but,
though such contact was capable of a thousand varia-
tions, its bounds were immovably fixed. Henry Adams
was an aristocrat, and a peculiarly modern aristocrat:
the tame and squeamish product of London or Boston,
quite unlike his spacious Renaissance ancestor for whom

privilege meant an extension, not a curtailment, of adventures.

This is palpable everywhere through the "Education"; but something else about Henry Adams is palpable in its very title. Adams self-consciously sought to channel his experiences and to convert them into education. The attitude is praiseworthy enough, but at the outset it is interesting to note what produced it. What first of all produced it, we may suppose, was his Puritan background, quivering with moral earnestness: a background which, moreover, if it served as a spur to education, served equally as a backstop; and which, if it accounts during four generations for the Adams strength, accounts no less for its want of suppleness. But the Puritan impulse coincided perfectly with something else which caused Adams to treat life as education: the nineteenth-century crusade for progress and enlightenment. The nineteenth century seemed to think that if man only knew enough, and remained a "moral" animal, he could reform and stabilize the world. The belief was hardly one which Adams, as he grew older, was encouraged to share; but the atmosphere that produced it was one he never outgrew. It was a moral as well as an intellectual impulse that caused him to plunge headlong into the flood of science and philosophy that engulfed his age; it was some desperate faith in pure knowledge, which even a highly ironic temperament could not extinguish, that turned Henry Adams into a lifelong student. True enough, it was difficult for him to make something systematic and cosmic of all he studied. The result, in that line, was never much more than brilliant dilettantism; but it saved Adams, if not from disillusionment, then from disintegration.

If the "Education" were no more than a worldling's reminiscences and a student's recapitulations, all tied together with philosophical ribbons, we might praise its prose and wit and acknowledge its intellectual expressiveness of an era; but we should put it among the memorials, and not the textbooks, of American experience. But the "Education" is a grand-scale study of maladjustment, of the failure of an exceptional personality to mesh with a prodigious civilization: posing, with one gesture, the problem of the man and his times. The problem of each, by the time Adams's autobiography was made public, had grown greater and more acute; so that in the decade following Adams's death the "Education" had a significance it only partly had in his lifetime and that there is small likelihood it will ever have again.

## II

Like most serious autobiographies, the "Education" is an attempt, not to record a man's life, but to explain it. It is the work, at bottom, of one who set out both to judge and to justify himself. This dual intention is significant, even though what Adams attempted to justify was failure. We may take the liberty of supposing that this dual intention was embodied very simply: Adams judged himself by asking a question, and justified himself by returning an answer. Why—he asks in effect—should someone who started off with every opportunity, and with faith and eagerness, have ended up with so little achieved, dissentient and in utter flight? Because, he answers, the world he had set out to serve had been seized by forces he would not accept for master; and nothing better remained than to try to understand those forces and inveigh against them.

The "Education" is, then, a perfectly *conscious* study of frustration and deflected purpose; of the failure of a superior man to find the right place, or any tolerable place, in a civilization growing ever more corrupt, rapacious and vulgar. No one ever wrote a more deliberate apologia of his life than Henry Adams. I shall have much to say later concerning the make-up of the particular man, concerning his blunders and prejudices, his distaste for enduring his situation, his predisposition to abandon it. But all that has a psychological importance, not a philosophical one; it delimits, but does not destroy, the real meaning of his book. What gives the "Education" its lasting value, what made a generation of futilitarians clasp it to their breasts, is the validity of the predicament regardless of the shortcomings of the man. For if not Henry Adams, then another, or many others, were paralyzed by the terms of that struggle in which he was so centrally engaged. Confronted by the greed of a banking civilization, the crookedness of boss-rule politics, the vulgarity of a parvenu culture, the cynicism of an exploitative ruling class, the middle-class intellectual was pretty well doomed either to suffer or succumb or escape. At the best, if his convictions had real fiber, he might die fighting the reformer's luckless battle; more likely he would accept the situation, as John Hay did, and wax fat off the spoils; or flee it and accept its more graceful counterpart elsewhere, as did Henry James; or take to excoriating it, aware that his mockery was the sign of his weakness, as Adams felt driven to do.

There appeared, in any case, to be no lasting adjustment that could be called an honest one. The superior man might, by the world's standards, succeed or fail; it hardly mattered, since he could not remain whole. No doubt he best avoided contamination by going into retirement; but then he was not fully alive, and then he had abandoned his responsibilities. If he remained in action, he might deceive himself into thinking that he was fighting the good fight by opposing specific men, by championing specific measures; but if he remained in action and refused to deceive himself, he knew he had for enemy the whole huge mass of things. And unless one was an incorrigible idealist or a convinced revolutionary, that was a task leading to dislocation and despair. Henry Adams, very early, became too pessimistic and cynical to go on being a participant. He chose, instead, a place on the sidelines, and from there set about recording the minutes of all the unsavory transactions of America's public life. The picture of such proceedings which Adams drew, or at least suggested, in the "Education" is a final one. For not only were its revelations damning, but its sources were unimpeachable. It was the indictment of a supremely placed worldling who had listened at the most private keyholes, who had been told—or allowed to guess—the secrets of those who worked behind the scenes. Scarcely anyone else who did so little knew so much. Adams's indictment stands: the great documentary merit of the "Education" is its demonstration of what nineteenth-century America had become, and by what process, and on what terms.

The philosophical merit, which once seemed a merit so much greater, is by no means so great. For the intellectuals of the twenties, the "Education" was an epic after their own hearts. *Epic* is no idly used word; the scale and severity of the book are important. In one sense, the most misleading thing about it is its impressiveness. Written with much of the formality that Gibbon used in his "Memoirs," it comes at the reader with so magisterial an air that halfway through it he grants it the confidence reserved for an attested masterpiece. The Adams manner confers on the Adams apologia a definite extrinsic weight. There is the sense of a large mind and an imposing personality; there is the sense—unimpaired by the irony of the book—of deep purpose and high seriousness. Henry Adams, who lived his life in a minor key, took every precaution to write about it in a major one. The "Education" is a completely full-dress performance.

The 1920's could use such an authoritative approach. The 1920's could bend the knee before a master who celebrated their own misgivings and disappointments. He ennobled their dilemma. He gave dignity to their frustration. For theirs was the individualist's dilemma, and for them the idea of integrity involved the idea of withdrawal; environment, to them, defeated the artist, as participation corrupted the thinker. Their dilemma, too, sprang from personal weakness no less than from social disorder. The "Education" gave to the 1920's, not the signal to fight but the leave to withdraw, by revealing how a better man had got waylaid and misplaced, had been passed up and slurred over and left to go unsung; for surely there is something in the tone of the "Education" that suggests, as not the least of the nineteenth century's blunders, its failure to recognize the worth of Henry Adams. On its lowest level, there is an immense amount of self-pity in Adams's book. On their lowest level, there was an immense amount of self-pity in the futilitarians of the twenties. Deep called unto deep.

But at another level there was something in the "Education" to make it one of the justly pivotal books of its era. It may express futility, but its tone is not wholly negative; there is something affirmative in it. And what it affirms is a toughness of mind, a quality of searching, weighing, testing, of coming to clear-eyed conclusions about the nature of things. Above all, it sets forth a mind and morality that spurned the optimistic and opportunistic formulas, from Emerson's down, that had made of American life such a shallow, shifty, spurious thing. At least the *idea* of education which Adams, solitary and recusant, imposed upon himself, was an exemplary idea. What Adams signifies at his best is unadulterated and grown-up thinking. This was something that his pupils of the twenties, groping backward in American letters—stumbling over the confusions of the Transcendentalists, the rampant Americanism that mars the democratic fervor in Whitman—could not easily find elsewhere. No wonder, then, that they thought they had found more than they actually did.

III

For impressive as the "Education" is, and definitive as is its mood, it somehow is not profound. It befits very few of us to condescend to Adams on the score of his cultural background, his political knowledge, his cerebral weight; but the fact remains that it is not for his "discoveries," or his clarifications of the human struggle, that we can seek him out. Those celebrated later chapters of the "Education"—The Dynamo and the Virgin, A Dynamic Theory of History[1]—are superb intellectual exercises, but it is hard to believe that they offer a synthesis which is more than personally brilliant and picturesque. When Adams looked to the past, for example, it was originally in search of perspective. He set about contrasting twelfth-century "unity" with twentieth-century "multiplicity," and the contrast is striking. But to what end? He conceived the earlier age as the better one, but must have known that it was impossible to return to it. The structure of twelfth-century life has no application in ours; the old wheels went round from a social force that had become inoperative and spent. Yet, more and more in the manner of an escapist, Adams tried to go back; there came to be more than an esthete's interest in his medieval studies, in the long twilit mystic spell of Chartres. Coldly judged, does not one pamper one's maladjustment by pining for what one cannot have?

There was nothing shallow about Adams's inquiry into human culture, either in its feeling or its facts; but it failed to produce any profound philosophy of life, even a profound skepticism. Adams knew too much, he knew (or thought he knew) too well whither things were drifting, he had—too arrogantly—a disbelief that any good could come of it, ultimately to profit from his career of "education." The philosophy he did evolve is understandable enough, and one must grant that there was a basis in experience for it. But it comes to no more than the pessimism of one who sees the world being ruined, and the cynicism of one who gives up trying to

---

[1]For which he was mainly indebted to his brother Brooks.

reclaim it. And in Adams there was also an uglier cynicism, of sitting back and watching the world, with a not
unmalign satisfaction, go to Hell. The motif of effort
and education which carefully governs Adams's autobiography tends to obscure this uglier cynicism; but
from a reading of the "Letters" one knows that it was
there, and one sees how, after a time, the moralist in
Adams gave up being in any sense a crusader and became a merely captious and querulous censor.

A crusader in the old Adams style Henry never was
at any time. In John and John Quincy Adams there
was little of Hamlet and much of Coeur-de-Lion; there
was the impulse, scarcely questioned, to act. Henry
never had that impulse. At the very outset of his career,
he thought rather of being *induced* to enter politics—
thought of his dignity as soon as his duty. The silver-
platter method failed, and in a way Henry would have
no other. It was not simply that he as proud as he
was ambitious, or as squeamish as he was moral; it was
that for a lifelong career in opposition the work was
too grubby, too dispiriting, too harsh, the odds against
winning were too fantastically high. The reformer who
would take on so forbidding a task needed to be something of a fanatic; and after all Henry Adams was
from the beginning the most sensitive of intellectuals,
the most cultivated of worldlings.

It would be absurd to imagine such a man becoming
a John Brown, a William Lloyd Garrison, a Debs. But
it would surely not be absurd to imagine such a man
becoming a Matthew Arnold. Each was born in the
shadow of a name outstanding for earnestness, each
was by temperament the reverse of a democrat, and
each grew up to find a place waiting for him in that

world where society and intellect, art and politics, meet. There may have been a decisive difference in the fact that Arnold had a living to earn, and Adams did not. But Arnold was not self-indulgent and Adams was; so that Arnold became the embattled foe of what seemed to him the powers of darkness, and Adams merely their bitter and acidulous historian. (It only counts against Adams the more that he understood the issues in a far wider sense than Arnold understood them.) There was something in Adams which, though it might have borne the arduousness of high public office, balked at the indignities of Arnold's private campaigning. By Adams's strongly developed eighteenth-century standards of worldliness, Arnold was doubtless a little plodding, a little ridiculous. He called Arnold the most honest man he knew, but he was never driven to accept the burdens of such an honesty. It was his Chesterfieldian sensibilities that largely ruined Adams; that turned him into a man who thought one way and lived another.

For he lived, during many years, in elegant and patrician retirement, choosing for his intimates the Hays, Cabot Lodges, Theodore Roosevelts for whom morally he had no respect; traveling *en prince;* entertaining *en connaisseur;* parading in his letters a calculated snobbery that sneered at Stevenson's indigent bohemianism, that instantly seized on Kipling's social second-rateness, that inveighed half to the point of mania against the Jews. He said of himself that he "should have been a Marxist," and knew, overwhelmingly, that he could never have been one. The whole story is told, I think, by Adams's reactions to English upper-class life. With his mind he saw all too well its hypocrisy, insularity, complacence; but temperamentally the sweetest air he ever breathed was that of London dinner-parties and English country houses.

The present moment is not congenial, and not disposed to be fair, to the "Education." The book compels respect for a sense of weight behind, not in, it. It suggests tragedy; but it is not—at least on the terms it set out to be—tragic, because the author chose the less costly form of defeat, and the less noble. Impotence, to Adams, was preferable to mutilation. Psychologically—by which I mean that were Henry Adams the problem of a novelist—his life followed a convincing pattern. But in real life, an ultimate failure of character is not to be excused by being explained; nor does a lifetime of self-analysis compensate for a failure to see things through morally. If a crude capitalist era "crushed" Adams, it was as much from being enervated by the fruits of it as from being poisoned by its roots. Was Adams willing—was he ever willing—to lose just part of the world to gain his own soul? It is just possible to say Yes; but if so, Adams's reason was purely pride.

However great the merits of the "Education," its "method' can already be seen to have failed. Culture and education are of the highest importance—according to some philosophies, the very end of living. But for Henry Adams they were clearly intended to be a means, carrying him forward to a better understanding and fulfillment of his obligations. Instead, they produced in him the indecision of a Hamlet; they became a kind of luxury, a kind of solace, and a kind of escape. It may be that Adams has taught us more in autobiography than he could have in action. It is at least certain that he has warned us more unforgettably. For it is not from confusing the mind by overloading it; it is not from dissent without protest, or opposition without strife, or humanism without humanity, that the beleaguered intellectual can save himself, or that the world he views with horror can be saved.

# III.

# Turner's "The Frontier in American History"

By CHARLES A. BEARD

FREDERICK JACKSON TURNER was born in Portage, Wisconsin, on November 14, 1861. He was educated in the local schools and at the University of Wisconsin, from which he was graduated in 1884. He received his Ph.D. from Johns Hopkins in 1890. His doctoral thesis, on the Indian trade of his native state, showed that he had already chosen the line of inquiry that he would follow all his life. He taught at the University of Wisconsin from 1889 to 1910. This was his most creative period—creative in thought, not in literary production, for he published only one book, "The Rise of the New West" (1906), which he contributed to the American Nation Series.

In 1893, at a meeting of the American Historical Association held at the World's Fair in Chicago, he had read his paper on "The Significance of the Frontier in American History." It was several times reprinted by historical societies, but did not appear in a book by Turner until 1920, when he published a collection of essays called "The Frontier in American History." In 1910 he accepted a professorship at Harvard, where he remained until 1924. Because of ill health he went to California, settling in Pasadena, where he was appointed research associate of the Huntington Library. Another volume of his essays, "The Significance of Sections in American History," was published in 1932, the year of his death, and was awarded the Pulitzer Prize in History. "The United States, 1830–1850," a volume that he never quite completed, was edited by Avery Craven and published in 1935.

ONE JULY DAY in 1893, members of a learned society heard a young man in Chicago read a paper which was destined to have a more profound influence on thought about American history than any other essay or volume ever written on the subject. The young man was Frederick Jackson Turner and the paper was entitled "The Significance of the Frontier in American History." Of course no one can prove that its influence has exceeded that of any other essay or volume on American history, but doubtless a consensus of competent opinion would support this proposition.

The young author of the learned paper was at the time engaged in teaching history in the University of Wisconsin. He was, indeed, a true son of that state, born in 1861 at Portage, on the upper agricultural frontier, educated at local schools, and graduated from the University at Madison. His father, Andrew Jackson Turner, an immigrant from Plattsburg, New York, is described by Frederic Paxson as a journalist, a politician and a local historian. Aided by his wife, Mary Hanford Turner, Andrew gave his son the best of training that his wit and the circumstances could afford. At all events, on the frontier where the youthful Frederick spent his early life, a heritage of Eastern culture was kept alive amid the rude environment of forest, field and petty village.

Entertaining the ambitions of many a Western boy, the young Frederick first thought of taking up journalism and elocution as a career, but was turned aside to the serious study of history, probably under the influence of his teacher, William F. Allen, and his friend, Reuben Gold Thwaites, head of the State Historical Society. From Wisconsin Turner went to Johns Hopkins University, then the outstanding center for graduate studies in America, and took his doctor's degree, offering a dissertation on the Indian trade in his native state.

Like the frontier on which Turner was born, Johns Hopkins University must have made its impression on his thinking. In 1890, when he came up for his degree, the historical department was largely dominated by German methodology and by one of the weirdest delusions that has ever afflicted American intellectual life, namely, the Teutonic theory of history—the theory that the Teutonic race has been the prime source of political liberty and popular government and that the roots of Anglo-Saxon democracy are to be traced back to tun-moots of barbarians in the forest of northern Germany. That Turner never surrendered to this form of historical necromancy seems certain, but it is not irrelevant to suggest that, as conceptions of ways of life, the idea of German forest liberty is not remote from the idea of frontier liberty in America.

However that may be, Turner went back from Johns Hopkins to teach at the University of Wiscon-

sin, and remained there until 1910, when he accepted
a call to Harvard. Owing in no small measure to his influence, during his years at Wisconsin, graduate work
in the humanistic studies, especially history, rose to a
position of first rank. Though the number of his graduate students was not large, it included a few scholars
of decided talent, and their indefatigable labor, coupled
with that of other students attracted by Turner's thesis, helped to spread his historical conception broadcast
in America. It was, in fact, through their publications
rather than his own work after 1893 that his thesis
was elaborated and disseminated. After delivering his
memorable address at Chicago, Turner confined himself to special researches and meticulous mapping of
sections. He wrote one volume for the American Nation Series, brought out a collection of his papers in
1920, another in 1932, and left an uncompleted manu-
script on the middle period of American history at
his death that same year; but he was not a voluminous
writer. He never added materially to the thought expressed in the Chicago address of 1893, although a
revolution was taking place in European historiography
between that year and the close of his life. At the age
of thirty-two Turner had matured his conception of
American history and given it to the world. That was
in truth enough for one man to do in a lifetime.

Personally Turner was one of the most modest and
diffident scholars ever produced in America. He had
none of Macaulay's "oracular arrogance" and he had
"the presentiment of eve." The renown that came to
him never turned his head. If anything it made him
more cautious, and more critical in examining his own
work. To students he was generous with his time and

strength. With friends he was always genial and eager to share his discoveries. Until the curtain of night fell, he was, like John Richard Green, engaged in the quest of learning. His rounded life was an ornament to American scholarship and to the republic from which it sprang.

II

The conception of American history which Turner presented at Chicago in 1893 contained twelve major elements: (1) "The existence of an area of free land, its continuous recession, and the advance of American settlement westward explain American development"; (2) "American social development has been continually beginning over again on the frontier"; (3) "The frontier is the line of most rapid and effective Americanization"; (4) "The frontier promoted the formation of a composite nationality for the American people"; (5) "The advance of the frontier decreased our dependence on England"; (6) "The legislation which most developed the powers of the national government, and played the largest part in its activity, was conditioned on the frontier"; (7) "Loose construction [of the Constitution] increased as the nation marched westward"; (8) "It is safe to say that legislation with regard to land, tariff and internal improvements—the American system of the nationalizing Whig Party— was conditioned on frontier ideas and needs"; (9) "This nationalizing tendency of the West . . . transformed the democracy of Jefferson into the national republicanism of Monroe and the democracy of Andrew Jackson"; "the most important effect of the frontier has been in the promotion of democracy here and in Europe. . . . The frontier is productive of individualism"; (10) "So long as free land exists, the opportunity for a competency exists, and economic power secures political power"; (11) "The frontier developed the essentially American traits—coarseness and strength, acuteness, inventiveness, restless energy, the masterful grasp of material things, lacking in the artistic but powerful to effect great ends"; (12) The closing of the frontier marked the close of "the first period of American history."

Although by the use of the terms "frontier" and "section" Turner lent some countenance to the idea that he was speaking of physical geography rather than social and economic arrangements in particular places and times, in fact in other essays, he made it clear that he had in mind class configurations—not mere forests, fields, cabins and regions. In another essay he said: "We may trace the contest between the capitalist and the democratic pioneer from the earliest colonial days." In a preface to O. G. Libby's work on the distribution of the vote on the Federal Constitution, published in 1907, Turner remarked that the study was a contribution to "an understanding of the relations between the political history of the United States and the physiographic, social and economic conditions underlying this history. . . . The economic interpretation of history has been neglected." In other words, Turner was primarily seeking to discover the economic conditions—including land tenure, opportunity to acquire a livelihood on the land, and hence personal security and independence—which had made possible, conditioned, if not determined, the growth of democracy in the United States.

Turner overemphasized, in my opinion, the influence of frontier economy on the growth of the democratic idea, on the formation of national policies and on constitutional interpretation. My grounds for dissent on this score are set forth in a review of his volume of essays, "The Frontier in American History," which was printed in The New Republic in 1921. It is unnecessary to repeat them here. Since that time other writers—for example, J. C. Almack, B. F. Wright and Louis Hacker—have attacked the general Turner thesis from various angles or visions. And the controversy still rages. To summarize the results would require a volume. To appraise them would be a herculean task.

At the moment, perhaps the most disputed point is the "safety value" theory ascribed to Turner, namely, the theory that cheap land in the West drew off industrial workers from the East, raised or prevented the lowering of wages there, eased the economic tension and slowed down the growth of the labor movement. On this subject hundreds of pages have been written pro and con. As to the upshot I confess many doubts. That a vast number of industrial workers personally escaped from "wage slavery" to "freedom" on the frontier does not seem to be established beyond dispute, but what the East would have looked like in 1850, 1870 or 1880 had there been no cheap land in the West is a problem which, I believe, historiography cannot solve. That the freehold farming system of the West did develop a peculiar type of democracy, did profoundly influence the course of American history, it seems to me, is now settled beyond question, largely through the labors of Turner and his students.

In fact this appears so obvious today that it may be wondered why Turner's paper of 1893 made such a furor. The explanation lies, partly at least, in the kind of histories which we had to read then. Nearly all of them were written in the East and South. We had Bancroft's bedizened history showing how hard God had worked to establish democracy of a thoroughly reputable variety in America. We had Hildreth's dry but realistic history which said relatively little about the West. We had Von Holst's mighty work on the slavery question—which Turner said "is an incident" in the history of the middle period. We had Schouler as an offset to Bancroft, and Alexander Stephens on the one, true and only interpretation of the Constitution. We had a few minor works which, as Henry Jones Ford once said, showed how civilization came into the United States by way of New England. We were, in fine, in the bondage of iniquity and the gall of bitterness—at least in the Middle West where I lived at the time Turner read his address at Chicago in 1893. And in the East the enlightened denizens, besides having their own history done to suit themselves, read in Edward Eggleston's "Hoosier Schoolmaster" that all of us beyond the Alleghenies, if not the Hudson, were almost, if not quite, uncouth savages. It is in some such setting that Turner's work appeared to be little short of epoch-making—as in fact it proved to be, both in conception and technique.

### III

One of the problems that has always troubled me in this connection is how Turner happened to come upon his conception. When I saw him from time to time I was so interested in the maps he was making or the new materials he had excavated that I never thought to ask him this leading question. He might well have hit upon the idea in Daniel Webster's speeches. Webster on more than one occasion declared that the clue to popular institutions and self-government in America lay in the abundance of cheap land, widely distributed among owners, freed from the military and feudal tenures which bound people to the soil in the Old World. It was this condition, he said, which "fixed" our frame of government and served as the foundation of the Republic from earliest times. When this equality is destroyed and property tends to accumulate in a few hands, Webster reasoned, then either a leveling revolution or a military dictatorship is to be expected. Jefferson also entertained similar views respecting the influence of cheap land on democracy. So did Madison and many other prime thinkers of older times. Was it from them or from other sources, including Achille Loria and L. Q. C. Lamar, that Turner caught the glimpse which served as a guide to his work? His essay of 1893 does not answer the question.[1]

Another problem that puzzled me in relation to the development of Turner's thesis, as I watched it through the years, was the long neglect of the democratic im-

---

[1]After this chapter was printed in The New Republic, Mrs. Zara Jones Powers, of the Yale University Library, drew my attention to an article by Wirt Armistead Cate in The Journal of Southern History, November, 1935, entitled "Lamar and the Frontier Hypothesis," in which Turner's debt to Lamar is set forth. Like other authors, Turner was doubtless influenced by the writings and discussions of many persons interested in the common problem.

pulses in Eastern idealism, of the labor movement now so fully treated in the works of John R. Commons and his associates, of the great capitalistic forces so powerful from Alexander Hamilton's day onward, and of the planting system in the South—all conditioning and determining influences in American history, along with agrarian freehold economy. It is fair to say that Turner himself took the broader view, as indicated above, but his essay of 1893 did not reflect it. On the contrary, in that paper he said flatly that free land and the westward advance "explain American development," and his disciples, failing to heed fully his other warnings, overworked this categorical declaration and did not give due space to other features of American civilization, especially the planting and capitalistic aspects. How they could have read the Fathers and missed these considerations is for me among the seven wonders of American historiography.

Likewise overworked, in my opinion, was the "individualism" of the frontier, which has been seized upon by James Truslow Adams and others less sophisticated as a stick to beat the New Deal. I knew in my youth pioneers in Indiana who had gone into the county of my birth when it was a wilderness. My early memories are filled with the stories of log-cabin days—of community helpfulness, of coöperation in building houses and barns, in harvesting crops, in building schools, in constructing roads and bridges, in nursing the sick, in caring for widows, orphans and the aged. Of individuals I heard much, of individualism little. I doubt whether anywhere in the United States there was more community spirit, more mutual aid in all times of need, so little expectation of material reward for services rendered to neighbors.

After all, the most powerful socialistic movement that has shaken American politics was the Populist upheaval of the nineties, and it was mainly agrarian in origin and support—and it was in full swing at the very moment when Turner read his essay at Chicago in 1893. It is not impossible that the talk about individualism among intellectuals at that time stemmed from the vogue of Darwinism, Spencerism and Manchesterism rather than from the thoughts of dwellers on the frontier. J. Laurence Laughlin published, in 1884, his mutilated edition of John Stuart Mill from which he omitted all the humanism, while including all the greed and adding more of his own manufacture.

The intellectual atmosphere of 1893 was highly charged. The fight over the income tax was growing hotter. Chicago was entering the throes of a panic. The Pullman strike was only a year off. In a few months Eugene V. Debs was to be outdone by Grover Cleveland's soldiers and then thrown into jail. The Populists had served their notice on the country in 1892, and Bryan's "socialistic" and "communistic" hordes, as Joseph Choate regarded them, were gathering for the fray of 1896. When Turner was formulating his passages on frontier individualism, was he affected only by the historical records of old times and not at all by Darwin, Spencer and the vibrant discussions going on around him? We may legitimately wonder without being able to say positively.

Finally, did the closing of the agricultural frontier really make so much difference as Turner or his disciples imagined? Certainly not enough industrial work-

ers had gone there in the earlier times to prevent business panics, urban poverty, labor unrest and the kind
of distress which we have witnessed since 1890—the
cabalistic year. Look at the unrelieved misery of 1837
described in Horace Greeley's reminiscences, at the
bread riots in New York in 1857 and the strikes that
accompanied the depression of 1873–78.

On the whole, industrial labor has been no more
violent since the opening of the twentieth century than
it was when the mystic frontier was beckoning. During
the sorrows of the 1837 panic, citizens in Cincinnati
broke open a bank that had shut its doors on deposi-
tors and carried off all the movable property they
could get their hands on. None of the financial institutions that had looted the country in the grand days of
normalcy suffered any such drastic treatment at the
hands of outraged customers in the black days of 1933.

The freehold frontier did have a lot of influence on
American development, but how much and what kind
is still an open question for me. That it does not "explain" American development I am firmly convinced.
What does explain this development I leave to those
who can write history as it actually has been. Yet I
have no doubt that the elbowroom we have enjoyed
here, the rich treasures we have fallen upon, used and
misused, the freehold tenure in agriculture now rapidly
declining, and absence of great landlordism from huge
sections of the country, have given to expressions of
human nature in the United States some of the distinc-
tive features which we call American.

# IV.

## Sumner's "Folkways"

By JOHN CHAMBERLAIN

WILLIAM GRAHAM SUMNER was born in Paterson, New Jersey, on October 30, 1840, but was educated in the public schools of Hartford, Connecticut. In 1859 he entered Yale, where he made an excellent record both scholastically and socially. After his graduation in 1863, he went abroad to study for the ministry at Geneva, Göttingen and Oxford. He then spent three years teaching freshman subjects at Yale, before being ordained a priest of the Episcopal church. In 1869 he was assistant rector of Calvary Church, in New York City; from 1870 to 1872 he was rector of a church in Morristown, New Jersey. Although he was popular with his congregations, he was aware that his major interests were political and economic rather than theological; and he was glad to accept the chair of Political Economy and Social Science that had just been created at Yale. There he spent the rest of his career.

As a scholar, he was at first concerned with the defense of laissez-faire economics against government interference. To this period belong his monumental "History of American Currency" (1874) and his celebrated lecture on the Forgotten Man (1883). But after 1890 he began to work in anthropology and to make a wide study of the evolution of social institutions. "Folkways" did not appear until 1907, three years before his death, and it was not until 1927 that his system of sociology was formally published: in a four-volume work called "The Science of Society," edited by his student and successor, Professor A. G. Keller.

WHEN, IN RESPONSE to a letter of
inquiry, I jotted down the title of William Graham
Sumner's "Folkways" as one of the books that had
changed our minds, I was confident that I was list-
ing one of the obvious major influences on American
thought. A diligent search through the critical literature of the past quarter-century, however, has only
served to disillusion me: references to Sumner are
few and far between, if we discount the works of Yale
graduates. If Franklin D. Roosevelt had not misap-
propriated one of Sumner's titles in his "forgotten
man" speech, Sumner would today be the Forgotten
Man. He was even overlooked, or dismissed, by Vernon Parrington, the voluminous and presumably definitive historian of the "main currents" of American
thought. You will look in vain through the index to
Parrington's "The Beginnings of Critical Realism in
America" for any mention of "Folkways," and the only
Sumner that is listed is the crabbed Charles. A publish-

er's footnote to the passages devoted to Henry C.
Carey and Francis A. Walker, two half-forgotten
economists of the Gilded Age, does inform us that
Parrington considered including a third sub-section on
Sumner, but evidently decided against it. No reason
for the decision is offered, but Parrington briefly indi-
cates his opinion of Sumner in one sentence: ". . . from
Wayland to Sumner they [the political economists]
upheld the abstract principle of free competition; but
what they could do in other ways to appease the wrath
of the protectionists they did heartily. . . ."

Thomas Beer does, of course, do handsomely by
Sumner in "The Mauve Decade." "In this maze of intellectual timidity," wrote Beer, "William Sumner
emerges as a cold, ponderous groper, an Episcopal
clergyman who threw off his silk and became deliberately an analyst of society, and the last libertarian of
the nineteenth century in the United States. He was
born so early in the century that he conceived of the
practice of free speech as an inalienable right of the
American citizen, and education not as a species of
social drill for the sons of pretentious women, but as
education, an argument between the instructor and the
instructed. . . . In 'Folkways' ideas are hidden around
the bulk of a clumsy oratorical protasis and definitions
must be exhumed as fossils from the marsh of swollen
paragraphs . . . but he took the one stride that separated him from other American sociologists of the
period: he was able, finally, to assume an exterior view
of all societies. . . ."

If Sumner can properly be termed the founder of an
objective American sociology, then the joke is obviously
on Vernon Parrington. There is, however, an excuse,

if not a justification, for the critical neglect of Sumner. For "Folkways" is not so much a seminal document as it is a part of a tradition that received its first great impetus from Darwin, Wallace and Herbert Spencer in England. True, Sumner was the first American to treat the customs, the folkways, the philosophical notions, the *mores* and the religion of a people from the genetic, or functional, standpoint. And in so doing, he practically created the subject of sociology on these shores, whatever may be said to the contrary by the partisans of Columbia University's Franklin Henry Giddings.

"Folkways" can be read by the unphilosophical as an enchanting compendium of subjects as diverse as witchcraft and bundling. Manifestations of patriotism, the whole interplay of mutualism and competition in the struggle for existence, slavery, cannibalism, sexual customs, incest, abortion and infanticide, customs arising out of kinship, asceticism—there is scarcely a topic relating to human habits under every conceivable stress that Sumner does not illuminate by foraging through the capacious filing cabinet which he spent a lifetime filling. Sometimes the method of classification seems to lead nowhere in particular; Sumner, who had an extremely honest conception of himself as a scientist, was afraid of making premature generalizations. But the drift of the book is plain: the one great idea that you take away from "Folkways" is the idea of the relativity of cultures, the feeling that no custom or habit-pattern is right or wrong except in relation to a time and a place.

Naturally this idea is neither astounding nor shocking to one who has already habituated himself to the genetic approach through contact with Darwin, Taine,

Huxley—or, for that matter, Marx and Engels. The notion that manners, morals and philosophies derive not from revelation but from the adjustments made by people to external conditions was revolutionary in the 1880's; and Sumner had to win a long knock-down and drag-out fight with President Noah Porter of Yale before he could use Herbert Spencer in his classroom. But the great victory for the evolutionary and the functional approaches was won on the field of biology; and Sumner can be credited only with adapting the Darwinian scientific method to the study of human society. That is credit enough for any man; but it explains how Parrington could feel justified in giving some eight pages to John Fiske as a direct popularizer of the school of Darwin and Herbert Spencer and only one slighting reference to Sumner. Fiske's popular broker-role was, after all, the wider, no matter what the sons of Elihu Yale may prefer to think.

But Fiske was by all odds the shallower person— and it is one of the great blots on Parrington's record that he missed the total import of Sumner which, as we shall see, is wider than can be comprehended from a reading of "Folkways" or Sumner's books and essays that are limited to laissez-faire economics. The fact that *mores* has passed into the vocabulary of people who have never opened "Folkways" is sufficient evidence that Sumner, who rescued the word from the Latin dictionary, has had a pervasive, even if unnoticed, camphor-ball effect on the intellectual atmosphere of our times. If Sumner has been neglected by a younger generation which has fed on the genetic studies of Veblen, Beard and others whose works are under discussion in this book, the reason has fundamentally to do with standards of journalism, not philosophic worth. Veblen and Beard attacked specific problems in a specific way. "An Economic Interpretation of the Constitution" makes its point quickly; anyone can enjoy it and understand it. Sumner's "Folkways," which consists of a vast encircling movement on ideas once cherished by the Protestant churches of America and all good citizens, is subtler, more devious. But properly interpreted, "Folkways" is just as disturbing to the view that the Constitution was ordained of God as is the work of Beard, for it proves by induction that *all* effective rules for human guidance, including those written down on parchment, come out of the *mores,* which are brought into being by human animals pursuing—or mispursuing—their interests. Parenthetically, it may be remarked that Veblen, who studied under Sumner in New Haven in the eighties, very probably derived some of his ideas on conspicuous waste from Sumner. I have in mind specifically the Veblen passages on conspicuous waste in the field of education. Sumner's great campaign of the 1880's against Noah Porter and the classical Yale curriculum was an attack on the "leisure-class" training that exalted the notions "that what is useful is vulgar" and that "useless accomplishments define a closed rank of superior persons." The words are Sumner's own; and if they do not constitute the seed-pod from which burst the flower of Veblen's "The Theory of the Leisure Class" then coincidence is a remarkable jade.

There is, however, no use quarreling over priorities in ideas: the worth of a concept does not depend on authority, but on relevance, and the priority game can be worked on Sumner as well as on Veblen. If I had

been properly educated by, say, Robert Maynard
Hutchins in the contents of the "great books of the
world," I should, no doubt, have begun with the great
Victorian evolutionary thinkers and then jumped to the
specific applications of the functional approach in men
like Beard and Veblen. I should have first learned
about the influence of the frontier on American history—and American democracy—from Turner, not
from stray passages in "Folkways" and from Sumner's
magnificent essay on the relation of men to land
called "Earth Hunger." But, by sheer chance, I happened to grow up in New Haven, where the cult of
"Sumnerology" thrives. I had a father who divided
his college courses at Yale into two categories: those
taken with A. G. Keller—Sumner's apostle and literary
executor—and the rest, which were presumably a complete waste of time. Naturally I took in a good deal of
Sumner through the pores, and whether "Folkways" is
a primary or a "secondary" book has never mattered
very much to me. Sumner has been since my adoles-
cence not so much an author as a presence. And there
is no better way to understand him than to show him
against the background of New Haven, a Puritan-
Congregational town that has profited from the sweep
of American industrial life without ever being actually
in it to the extent of a Pittsburgh—or even a Water-
bury or a Bridgeport.

## II

Sumner's father, Thomas Sumner, an immigrant
from Lancashire, was one of those stubborn, self-taught
machinists who, in the early days of the last century,
haunted mechanics' institutions in search of knowledge.

Back of the father lay generations of weavers, "artisans and members of the wage class," as Sumner himself put it, whose "trade was ruined by machinery." The evils of early industrial capitalism, however, did not make Thomas Sumner class-conscious; they merely made him indefatigably self-sufficient. The year after William Graham was born in New Jersey, Thomas went on a prospecting trip to Pennsylvania and Ohio, but he returned with the conviction that life on a mechanic's wages in a settled community was preferable to pioneering in the wilderness. British phlegm and a habit of downrightness seem to have been the sometimes quarreling characteristics of the whole Sumner breed. And the "dogged-does-it" work methods of William Graham were obviously derived from Thomas.

The son was trained for the ministry at Yale, at Göttingen in Germany, and at Oxford, where he discussed Buckle and the "philosophy of history" with avidity in the expanding atmosphere of the mid-Victorian years. In England young students were wondering if it was possible to have a "science of society." But while the English were wondering, the German scholars were perfecting a fruitful method by applying the so-called Higher Criticism to the study of Biblical origins. Sumner was more impressed by the "nobly scientific" attitude of Göttingen than he was by anything at Oxford. Later he learned that the "social science of Germany is the complete inversion in its method of that of German philology, classical criticism and Biblical science. Its subjection to political exigencies works upon it as disastrously as subjection to dogmatic creeds has worked upon Biblical science in this country." With this distinction in his mind Sumner managed to escape what he termed the Hegelian "fever"; the magic formula of "thesis, antithesis, synthesis" meant nothing to him. Yet his German experience predisposed him to Darwinism quite as much as Hegel predisposed other schools of the mid-century to the theory of a continually evolving world.

Before the solvents of the Higher Criticism had worked to undermine his religious faith, Sumner was ordained a deacon and a priest of the Protestant Episcopal church. He became a rector in 1870, but found that when he came to write his sermons he tended to produce disguised tracts on social science and economics. When he was offered the chair of Political Economy and Social Science at Yale in 1872 (for a time there was a movement afoot to bring him back to New Haven as a professor of Greek!) he jumped at the chance. Exposure to Darwin, Huxley, Haeckel and Spencer produced an instantaneous reaction in him. As Keller points out in an affectionate memoir, Sumner's philological training enabled him to read Job, the "Odyssey," Virgil, Dante, Goethe, Ibsen, Dostoevsky, Sienkiewicz, Calderón, Molière and Camoëns all in the original, and the likenesses and differences in the customs of various "in-groups" and "out-groups" the world over were familiar to him through the study of comparative literature. Once given the clarifying lead of the evolutionary theory, the likenesses and differences in customs and laws began to make sense as what was "fittest to survive" under the widely varying conditions of the earth's surface.

But cultural relativity and New Haven did not wholly mix. Aside from the difficulties which Sumner had with Noah Porter, there was the dominant capitalist ethic which Sumner clung to unreservedly through thick and thin. New Haven has always been something of a *rentier* town; the university, which lives on endowments, makes that inevitable. The rawer phases of industrialism can, of course, be found if you look for them on East Chapel Street, or near the Winchester, the Marlin and the Acme Wire factories. But there were no blast furnaces, no Pullman strikes, no great disturbances in New Haven to disturb Sumner's pondering; and the Populists of the West, with their cheap-money clamor, could only seem ridiculous to him. Laissez-faire, when all is said, is convincing as an ideal, even though human beings seem constitutionally averse to letting it work out in practice. And it could only seem good to Sumner as he meditated on an expanding America in his somewhat aloof station in Lawrence Hall or during his late-afternoon rambles in the pleasant Ridge Road country out beyond East Rock.

It is at this point that Sumner begins to seem fallible and parochial like the rest of us, for all the legendary impressiveness of his "iron voice" and "magnificent baldness." For if human beings are averse to letting laissez-faire work its presumed magic, if "interests" insist on asking for protection and labor unions are by their very nature unwilling to let wage cuts take place "naturally," then there must be something in the *mores* that makes for such cussedness. Sumner frequently preached against the "absurd attempts to make the world over." Yet here he was, as a last-ditch champion of Adam Smith, trying to "make over" the average individual's habit of asking for governmental intervention to render the struggle for existence less harrying. If you comb "Folkways" you will find numerous instances of how Sumner's economic theology gets in the way of his scientific method. A truly objective sociologist will note that peoples, organized as national "in-groups," will sometimes prefer the security of a balanced economy to the higher standard of living that may be had from a specialized economy. The choice may not make sense to those naturally predisposed to getting the most goods for the least money. But if you have only one type of product to sell—as the island of England has only her finished goods—then you expose yourself to the depredations of any neighbor that can put itself athwart the lanes of supply by which you are accustomed to get other goods. Since "Folkways" teaches us that no human choice is eternally "right," Sumner's laissez-faire absolutism can only seem out of character with his profession as a social scientist. In any event, Sumner's disciples haven't been able to make head or tail of the world since the war; they envisaged no great repudiation of the philosophy of history that stressed a continually increasing world division of labor.

In one section of "Folkways" Sumner speaks of the decay of the Roman Empire. He writes: "The abuse of democratic methods by those-who-had-not to plunder those-who-had must also have had much to do with the decline of economic power, and with the general decline of joy in life and creative energy." Such a sentence is unbecoming to a "scientist," for it presupposes the law and says the facts "must" have fitted the rule. A perfectly good case could be made out that the converse of Sumner's statement was true, and that the decline of economic power preceded and "caused" the plundering of the "haves" by the "have-nots." In fact,

Henry George made out just such a case in "Progress and Poverty" long before "Folkways" finally saw the light of publishing day in 1907. George traced the decline of Roman economic power to the hogging by the rich of the available productive land. Sumner was perfectly aware, as "Folkways" shows, of the great Roman latifundia, or slave-worked estates. And he was certainly aware of Henry George; indeed, he was wont to criticize him. The connection between monopoly and poverty never seemed real to Sumner, who was sure that capitalists would invest their money in ways that might be counted on to maximize production if only government "jobbery" could be eradicated. But there was the rub: the *mores* derive from the pursuit of "interests," and capitalist short-run interest is frequently against laissez-faire and on the side of "jobbery." To hope for a "perfectly" meshing capitalist system, with everyone pursuing the "long-run" interest of all, is as idealistic as to hope for socialist perfection, and Sumner is hoist by his own petard.

### III

Sumner's economic conservatism naturally made him an enemy of the revolutionists of his day. But revolutionists ought to listen to him. No one will ever be surprised, after reading "Folkways," at the spectacle of Thermidorian reaction following upon revolution; the *mores* are stubborn and as slow to change as the elephant is to mate, and the edicts of a Robespierre and a Trotsky can have only a slight effect on them. But revolutionary sweeps do have permanent effect, for all that. The marital customs of the French peasant may be more or less today what they were in the eighteenth century. But no French peasant who dates his freehold to the Great Revolution will tell you that the "Marseillaise" was sung for nothing.

Sumner is justified in his contempt for the more Utopian revolutionaries, but he often misses the point that revolutions can change things from the economic standpoint. The French Revolution was, of course, an individualist's revolution, and Sumner might justify its gains as illustrative of the principles he thinks to be relatively sound. But communalism, if not communism, can be a mode of life; and Margaret Mead has aptly demonstrated the extreme elasticity of the human animal by her investigations of primitive communal and individualist cultures that sometimes exist almost within a stone's throw of each other. In using Sumner as a stick with which to belabor New Deal "interventionist" economics as "socialistic," A. G. Keller no doubt carries on as the Master would require. But that is not the scientific approach: the *mores* all over the world are sanctifying the "interventionist" state. And it is useless, on Sumner's own evidence, to buck the *mores* head on: if one aspires to leave an impress on one's time one can only hope to give a slight twist to events. Statesmen who fail to "gauge forces in the *mores* and to perceive their tendencies" (the words are Sumner's own) are blown away.

But Sumner's weak points are, after all, the weak points of an age; his strength, on the other hand, lives on. Social-science methods have become far more rigorous and precise since the publication of "Folkways," and the field expedition has replaced Sumner's reliance on the printed word and the traveler's tale. Yet every anthropologist and sociologist "on location" owes a debt to Sumner's attempted "exterior view." And, for those of us who are merely looking for the "idea of the thing," the text of "Folkways" is still the most powerful general compendium of the *mores* that may be obtained. Read once, however, it can be placed upon the shelf to gather dust. For it is not a charming book; its prose is the prose of an old man who hated the agonies of composition. It is in his shorter essays that Sumner shows to best advantage as a stylist. The peroration of his "The Conquest of the United States by Spain," written when the post-1898 imperialist fever was at its height, is a plea for isolation from the troubles of the Old World that rings truer than ever today. Firmly grounded in a knowledge of the *mores* of our once Jeffersonian Republic, it is one of the noblest pieces of polemical writing in the language.

# V.

# Veblen and "Business Enterprise"

By R. G. TUGWELL

THORSTEIN VEBLEN was born in Cato Township, Wisconsin, on July 30, 1857, the sixth of twelve children of a couple who had emigrated from Norway. When he was eight his family moved to Minnesota, where he was brought up on a farm in a Norwegian district. At seventeen he went to Carleton College, spending three years in the preparatory school and three more in the college proper, from which he was graduated in 1880. For a year he taught at Monona Academy in Madison, Wisconsin; then he went East to do graduate work, first at Johns Hopkins and afterwards at Yale, where he studied philosophy under President Noah Porter and social theory under Sumner. He earned his board by teaching in a military academy, lived alone, was despised as a foreigner and an agnostic. He received his Ph.D. in 1884, but found no teaching post, so he returned to his family's Minnesota farm for seven years.

In 1891 he went to Cornell to do more graduate work and was befriended by J. L. Laughlin, who brought him to the Economics Department of the University of Chicago, the following year, as a fellow. By 1900 he had risen to the rank of assistant professor. In 1899 he published his first book, "The Theory of the Leisure Class"; in 1904 came "The Theory of Business Enterprise." From 1906 to 1909 he served as an associate professor at Stanford, and from 1911 to 1918 at Missouri, where he gave the great course on "Economic Factors in Civilization" from which came his book, "The Instinct of Workmanship" (1914). In 1918 he quit academic life, becoming an editor of The Dial and a lecturer at the New School for Social Research. His most revolutionary writings were the product of this last period—"The Higher Learning in America" (1918), "The Vested Interests and the State of the Industrial Arts" (1919), "The Engineers and the Price System" (1921) and the papers on the war and the Bolshevik Revolution. He died on August 3, 1929.

V EBLEN WAS A STRANGE CREATURE, looked at through common-sense eyes; and commentators have not known quite how to account for the distillation into so alien a vessel of an American century's discontents. At any rate he remained a stranger; when conciliatory gestures were made in his direction he chose to ignore them. This went to extremes; an outright offer, ultimately—which came from the conservatives by way of reparation—to make him President of the American Economic Association was languidly refused. Of course that was very late and by then he had become a persistent concealer of prides as well as sorrows behind a mask of indifference. How much that presidential offer meant there is no evidence to show; but there is plenty to show that secretly he had no doubt of his own superiority, although unpleasant experience had taught him the folly of revealing it. Indeed, it was the fear of ridicule that caused him to adopt the mask of irony and indifference he wore throughout life.

All this was not apart from his work; it is, indeed,

of unusual importance that these personal factors as well as the conceptional framework within which he operated should be understood. This kind of analysis perhaps ought never to be neglected; but Veblen is so often pictured as a disembodied intelligence that exploration of his devious relations with the world is doubly necessary. The fact is that none of our social philosophers has been more genuinely part of the events of his time. He was shaped by and helped to shape his environment as few men are able to do. No one now doubts his power; not so many understand that its source lay in an anger which was diffused beneath a crusted surface.

His smoldering animus is easily understood if it is kept in mind that he came of foreign peasant stock and that he grew up in the Midwest of the seventies and eighties. A Norwegian sense of superiority together with an inevitably inferior status as one of an immigrant family; a self-respecting farmer's individualism together with resentment at exploitation by Yankee village traders; a scholarly bent together with maddening ineptitude, well into adult life, with English; an agnostic temper together with rigidly orthodox discipline, economic, moral, religious—these conflicts within and without ravaged him as an individual, and they certainly help to explain his mordant emphasis on the paradoxical elements in social change. No one knowing his experience would expect him to have judged the world good or the forces working in our culture meliorative. And it was his sidling tactical approach to a hostile world, also, which determined that his method should be analytic and roundabout, rather than forthright and advisory.

It would be difficult to say which of his books influenced us most. "The Theory of Business Enterprise" was more closely related to the formation of public policy. But it was the third of a trilogy in which "The Theory of the Leisure Class" came first, and a series of articles which included "The Preconceptions of Economic Science" second. All these, as can be understood from unmistakable likenesses melting into and illuminating one another, emerged from the same mind during one period of an uninterrupted stream. So that if one book cannot be centered on, one creative design is quite easy to distinguish. The effort resulted in a system—and it was a system which, in spite of its incompatibility with instrumentalism, a whole generation of instrumentalists has used. It evidently formed, for an age of science, an (economic) hypothesis more attractive than any suggested alternate; and from its first enunciation of a new method the decay of economic classicism set in. After its original drafting, in the very early years of the century, it underwent no basic change; the framework and the apparatus were simply turned to expanded uses. Later works—such as "The Engineers and the Price System," "The Higher Learning in America," and so on—were not different in a philosophical sense; they were applications of a method already developed.

To say which of his books was most important would require separation of method from hypothesis. In such a philosopher as Mr. John Dewey method is all-important; in Veblen that is not so certain. It would be difficult to say whether institutionalism was used to arrive at the theory (and perhaps to establish it as more than hypothesis) or whether it was conceived as having a value unrelated to a particular end. And it may be, of course, that Veblen did not distinguish, though that seems doubtful in view of his philosophical training under good masters and of his aptitude for metaphysics. At any rate both method and hypothesis have influenced all of us, and not necessarily together.

To the unwary, Veblen has seemed to have created his system almost as a by-product of something which to him was important, reaching a new economics by way of the conspicuous consumption illustrated in women's dress, or by way of economists' neglect for their subject matter—which, he said, was business and the machine process—in favor of taxonomic exercise. The studies in deliberate waste seemed to have been animated by a racial bitterness, and the undermining of economics by the need for intellectual revenge. Both have been ascribed to compensatory compulsion. Before he got through, however, it began to appear that he had done something more important than merely to exercise a complex. Those who put it all together could infer an intention to expose capitalism as an impossible mixture of mutually canceling elements, and the going economics as an inferior example of the artificial one-thing-at-a-time method. Certainly to the casual student the hypothesis was everything; to others the new institutional method had the value of release from orthodoxy and was therefore far more important.

II

The machine process, which was the beating heart of modernism, set up a discipline, Veblen said, which called for one set of traits—exactitude, faithfulness to

standards, subjection to rhythm, steadiness—to keep it
going; but it was operated by businesses which enforced
habits of the opposite sort—speculation, sportsmanship, conspicuous consumption, wasteful ceremonial,
whimsical management.

Received economics served to conceal this paradox,
it appeared, by never reasoning about the operating
world, only about an assumed one in which men re-
sponded automatically to a calculation of pleasures as
against pains, and in which prices reflected degrees of
willingness to serve or to sacrifice. Economics was like
a neglected religion in this, that it had nothing to do
with the behavior of men on weekdays—only, so to
speak, on economic Sundays.

The inference embedded in this was that any positive
rationale lay in men's natures and in their working
lives. "The Theory of the Leisure Class" explored the
one and "The Theory of Business Enterprise" elaborated the other—but always negatively and with much
left to the imagination. Both books began with
majestically simple propositions, from which they arrived at their outrageous conclusions by the statement
of other simple propositions following each other with
deceptive under-emphasis; the piling up of the load was
so neat as to be almost unnoticed. "The Leisure Class,"
which established the method, began, for instance, by
noting the emphasis on class distinctions at the higher
stages of barbaric culture—as in feudal Europe or
Japan—and going on to observe how the upper classes
were exempted from industrial occupations and reserved for activities to which honor attached; it was
merely remarked that these had to do largely with
fighting and exploiting. This thesis ran on and elabo-

rated itself in a wholly unobjectionable fashion until
the next was about to appear, whereupon it was disclosed that arrival had been made at a decisive stage:

> . . . no employment and no acquisition is morally possible
> to the self-respecting man except . . . to kill, to destroy such
> competitors in the struggle for existence as attempted to resist
> or elude him . . .

This was modern man, not his ancestors!

The argument here rested upon an anthropological
view for which no evidence was adduced, just as the
opening argument of the "Business Enterprise" rested
also upon a statement of the nature of business and of
modern work which was unsupported. Each of these
generalities carried a vast superstructure of theory;
each must have been prepared with appalling labor
and rigorous thought over many years. Arrogance of
simplification could scarcely have been carried further.
It illustrates that contempt for his readers which was
instinct in every line of Veblen, along with a contrasting care for meeting standards of his own.

An even more flagrant example followed. For the
second theme in "The Leisure Class" lifted out of the
heart of a wholly implied psychological system an "instinct of workmanship" which was to be basic. Veblen
let it go at this:

> As a matter of selective necessity, man is an agent. He is, in
> his own apprehension, a center of unfolding impulsive activity
> —teleological activity. He is an agent seeking in every act the
> accomplishment of some concrete, objective, impersonal end.
> By force of his being such an agent he is possessed of a taste
> for effective work, and a distaste for futile effort.

Before the introduction to "The Leisure Class" was
complete, social forces had been ranged in fateful op-

position: the exploitative and competitive against the peaceable and industrious, the hunter-warrior against the settled workman—that is to say, business against industry, pecuniary emulation against the instinct of workmanship. And if any reader had not followed, he was at liberty to quit. No writer like this could possibly have had numerous readers. This need not make him any less well known, of course. Eager popularizers were at hand. . . .

### III

It is important to notice that both themes—the one resting on anthropology and the other on psychology— were introduced in Darwinian terms. The first mentioned survival in a struggle for existence, the other a "selective necessity." The institutionalism was, when he arrived at it, cast also in evolutionary terms, standing thus opposed to the pre-Darwinian economic classicism.

"The Leisure Class," it could finally be seen, was not important because of its quotable contempt for modern wasters, but because it explained the existence of standards and of conformities which made such pitiable fools of men and women. Selectivity operated to produce a result which might, under other circumstances, have been reversed. Veblen was certainly not averse to ridiculing the business classes; he did, however, have a deeper purpose in showing how they had descended from a barbaric strain; his interest lay in the paradox of their duties, not in the objects under examination. The institutional theory was elaborated thus:

The life of man in society, just like the life of other species, is a struggle for existence, and therefore it is a process of selective adaptation. The evolution of social structure has been a process of natural selection of institutions. . . . Institutions are not only themselves the result of a selective and adaptive process which shapes the prevailing or dominant types of spiritual attitude and aptitudes; they are at the same time special methods of life and of human relations, and are therefore in their turn efficient factors of selection. So that the changing institutions in their turn make for a further selection of individuals endowed with the fittest temperament, and a further adaptation of individual temperament and habits to the changing environment through the formation of new institutions.

How this applied to the modern industrial culture was explained in "The Business Enterprise." The machine was the dominant institution in industry. Its routine set a pattern and pace to which all else must accommodate itself—if society was to live and prosper; but of course society need not live and prosper. For the proclivities of the destructive honor-men survived in the captains of business whose activities damaged the productive machine. The result of this conflict in disciplines, by which one class destroyed, wasted and even prevented the production of the commodities made by another class, was instability and periodic depression. The theory of credit and capitalization was worked out twice over to show that the creation of surpluses (or underconsumption if one preferred to put it that way) was a business fact, not an industrial one. An industrial system run by government (for instance) rather than by business would (inferentially) produce generously the right goods and services, and they would be used completely by consumers; business men lived by confusing what was essentially uncomplicated, by stopping and starting production, thus creating shortages and surpluses, by manipulating prices, and profiting by change. The rigging essential to this was done through the system of credit. What was capitalized was future profits; but profits were not dependent on productivity; they were perhaps oftener made by limiting it. Credit, therefore, further ensured instability.

When this theory was carried over into politics, government appeared also as a business institution. If it had been industrial it would have been forced long since to eliminate business as an agent of destruction. But the common-sense, non-reasoning approach of the ordinary citizen made it seem clear to him that what was good for business was good for himself, just as what once had been good for the Prince had also seemed good for the subject. This was the emulation principle at work. Public policy, in a state dominated by majority franchise, was therefore cast in favor of business and against industry—which meant the enforcing of insecurity and periodic collapse. Here was the common-sense mind laboring and producing its own destruction. Teleology operated, but it operated through institutions which implacably opposed each other.

## IV

The last chapter of "Business Enterprise" was devoted to the "natural decay" of the institution. This was the final irony. Historians before Veblen had pointed out that business had not exactly existed since the dawn of time and that its claim to sacredness was suspiciously recent. It remained for Veblen to suggest that it was not even the permanent end of a beneficent evolutionary process—that, in fact, its regime normally would be transitory. Business having come to its full development, he said, decomposition would set in quite naturally.

The machine process, as a discipline, acted to cut away the basis on which business enterprise was founded: the system of natural and property rights, of honorifics, of the wasteful use of goods, of elaborate ceremonial and the infantilisms of sportsmanship. It was of the nature of business, however, to eliminate competitors, in which case the whole complex of motivations tended to fail, since there were always fewer and fewer profit receivers and more and more wage-takers. For men who worked at routine jobs and who got no speculative gains were subject to the discipline of the machine process and did not respond to the stimulations of pecuniary emulation. Routine jobs in the industrial discipline multiplied inordinately as the consolidation of business enterprise went on; the time came, too, when enterprise was completely dependent on the machine process to get anything done; and when that happened all the inevitable decays of conflict must set in: "In their struggle against the cultural effects of the machine process . . . business principles cannot win in the long run; since an effectual mutilation or inhibition of the machine system would gradually push business enterprise to the wall." Business dared not kill the goose which laid the golden eggs even when it grew to monstrous size and refused submission to its master.

That something of another nature would result from regression of the modern culture was clear. What it might be was nowhere explicit. An elaborate scientific pose was Veblen's answer to those who inquired concerning the future. His was an analytical work, he replied, and he had no interest in prophecy. The inevitability of destruction was the unforgettable lesson. Of course there were very few at the century's beginning who quite believed it, or, for that matter, who believe it now, however complete their intellectual assent. That a theory can actually be true is hard to accept if it happens not to be acceptable anyhow. The political economy of Ricardo, Mill and Marshall was completely false if this was a genuinely operative principle; it was, indeed, no more than a justification—a screen for the nastier aspects of industrialism. If the persistent suicidal compulsion to which Veblen pointed were accepted, it followed that the end for capitalism must be death—perhaps by collapse, perhaps by slow self-strangulation; and this was the conclusion which it was so hard to accept.

During the decade following the war, doubters were laughed down and the Veblen cult was pretty well confined to a few *littérateurs*. The depression was a nasty shock for those who thought that a meliorative principle worked through the meanest tricks of competition to establish the best of all possible worlds; but the delusion, though its brightness was fogged, survived even that. It would not have surprised Veblen if someone had been able to tell him in his eighty-second year that the culture he had long since come to regard as doomed was marching rapidly down the secular curves of regress; it is even possible that he might not have been surprised to hear that the march was being accompanied by a desperately strident chorus of praise for the virtues he knew to be fatal ones. His own disillusions could only be measured, ever, by the contrasting illusions of his fellow men; for these were foster parents to the vultures of conflict which were tearing at the vitals of civilization.

v

It is not necessary to apologize now for making a cursory exegesis of what was a complicated logical structure. Years ago Mr. Joseph Dorfman completed that task in definitive fashion. The reader who cares to explore the apparatus is asked to read the fourteenth chapter of "Thorstein Veblen and His America." What Mr. Dorfman could not do once and for all—because a book has to stop somewhere and be published—was to trace out Veblen's widening influence as the years passed and to measure the march of events toward the conclusions he had anticipated. That had to be left for others.

Mr. C. E. Ayres observes, in his chapter on Mr. John Dewey, that he does not seem remarkable any more because his thought has passed into our minds and become familiar. This is almost as true of Veblen. The opening statement of "The Business Enterprise," describing the discipline of the machine and how it differed from the old enterpriser's rule of thumb, seems commonplace now; but that is because it has been so thoroughly accepted. It is only with something of an effort that it is recalled how little he had to go on in making this generalization. Taylor and scientific management were known then to a small circle of engineers, but probably no economist had heard of either—the name was not yet invented—and certainly none had seen that any modification of common sense was necessary. All that is not so strange or remarkable as the intellectual effort was, leading to the further generalization that concatenation was of the essence of the entire standardized industrial process. Taylor was still working at his simple time-and-motion studies; he had not yet written even the "Shop Management"; not until a few years before the war would he approach such an apprehension as Veblen had of the significance of series-operations. The theorist anticipated the experimenter by more than a decade. Yet, little as he had to go on, he was not afraid to make this a bearing foundation of his structure.

He went on to show how the system *at large* was taking on the character of "a comprehensive, balanced mechanical process" and to conclude that "any degree of maladjustment in the interstitial coördinations" was dangerous. But it was, he said, "by business transactions that the balance of working relations . . . is maintained or restored, adjusted and readjusted." And business men had no knowledge of a duty to coördinate; society held out to them rewards for preventing, equally with rewards for effecting, coördination. Many a Veblen student went back to read the closing sentence of that chapter, after 1929, wondering how he could have missed its meaning: "The larger and more close-knit and more delicately balanced the industrial system, and the larger the constituent units, the larger and more far-reaching will be the effect of each business move in this field." This, they could then see, was why 1929 was not an "ordinary" depression but a new phenomenon of a magnitude and range hitherto unknown.

There existed not only a technological tenuousness, but also a tenuousness of size. Yet Veblen was perfectly clear that mankind was committed to both by a relent-less evolutionary process, working not only through institutions but, as he had explained, through the teleologic necessity illustrated in the instinct of work-manship. He was never taken in by the current es-sentially reactionary progressivism; it was character-ized, it will be remembered, by "trust-busting" and attacks on Wall Street after the manner of the first Roosevelt, the elder La Follette and the muckrakers. Indeed, he pointed out that the big business man performed a useful function in destroying the little ones and thereby reducing the number of dangerous inter-ruptions to "interstitial coördination." It was true that, because of their independence of any control, they made crises more convulsive, but that was a matter of degree rather than of kind. He indicated later that this coördinative process might be turned over to a kind of Soviet of Engineers, if the captains of finance could be eliminated who created the pecuniary emulative stand-ard which traversed the workmanlike tendencies of industry.

## VI

Veblen's creative years—measured by consequence in the establishing of his system—began at Cornell and ended at Chicago. The years ran roughly between 1891 and 1906. The student period at Carleton, at Johns Hopkins and at Yale had, before his Cornell appoint-ment, been behind him for seven apparently shiftless years. In reviewing them and speculating on their rela-tion to the sudden outpouring which followed immedi-ately, one is inevitably reminded of the lazy Watt and the boiling kettle, or the young Newton idling under

the apple tree. Those stories must be folk-syncopations
of long and unsuspected gestations. Certainly no one
guessed, least of all his worried family, that Veblen
was carrying an equally amazing embryo during those
seven exasperating years of sheer idleness.

Comment has been made on the calm, sometimes in-
direct way in which the various themes of the theory
appeared and were woven together. The reasons for
this lay only partly in his bent for work; they lay partly
also in the kind of auspices under which it had to be
done. He had finally escaped from the discipline of the
plains; but American universities in general, and Cornell
and Chicago in particular, were hardly to be regarded
as breeding places for social invention. Indeed they
took considerable pains to insure orthodoxy. But the
President Harpers could not be everywhere and see
everything. At Chicago Harper felt himself safe
enough with a fellow brought from Cornell at the
instance of the ineffable Laughlin, whose belief in the
divine right of business was scarcely less than that of
George Baer.[1] Laughlin's sponsorship of Veblen is still
mysterious. It is, of course, entirely possible that the
older man never understood what his junior was driving at. That it was subversive, not merely ironical, did
not become clear to anyone for some time. Eventually
he was found out; but meanwhile he enjoyed his
scholarly opportunities.

His extended book reviews in The Journal of
Political Economy, which he edited for several years,

---

[1] It was Baer who, in the midst of the anthracite strike of 1901, wrote
to an inquiring clergyman that "the rights and interests of the laboring
man will be protected and cared for—not by the labor agitators but
by the Christian men to whom God in His infinite wisdom has given
the control of the property interests of the country. . . ."

his long technical articles, and finally his books, had a very limited audience. Even today that is true. Probably as many people read Newton's "Principia" or Darwin's "Origin" in any given year as read "Business Enterprise." When the lectures he made in his sleepy drawl to a handful of students, the book notes and reviews in obscure periodicals, the articles and monographs, were rewritten and appeared as the two first books, the author himself had to pay for their publication. Up to Veblen's death "Business Enterprise" had sold only about 4,000 copies. This did not make Veblen's life an easily independent one; also, like most social inventors, he had academic notoriety but no praise to speak of, and spent the years in a gathering cloud of suspicion. It did not help that his personal relations were irregular and disturbed. He had no close friends, perhaps because he so invariably turned a sneering face to the world, perhaps because he had one of those unpleasant, rather unclean appearances, as though he washed infrequently and neglected his clothing. Yet, though he had no friends, he seems to have appealed to a number of women—too many, considering that he needed to maintain a place in the ultra-respectable environs of the pre-war universities. Take him altogether: a theorist whose attack, sly and slow as it was, on the institutions of competitive capitalism, was the most dangerous ever made; an academic dweller who fouled the neat nest of economics with slurring doubts of his colleagues' intellectual honesty; an untidy disregard of conventions which were enforced by a campus-corps of idle women—it is remarkable that when Chicago cast him out he should successively have found refuge at Stanford and at

Missouri. Ultimately the academic world refused to tolerate him.

Ill and exhausted, his creative years far behind him, he approached an end which came in 1929. The last article he wrote was rejected for publication. This was in 1927. Mr. Dorfman records his answer to an inquiry, after this, as to why he wrote no more: "I am seventy years old," he said, "and I have decided not to break the Sabbath. It is such a nice Sabbath." This, too, was double-edged. Nothing was nice about that last Sabbatical which no institution had given him as a right. He was worshiped from afar by scattered students, but he had no one to talk with; he had most of his income from a former student as charity. The man who shook the world with his irony, and who opened the way to a new social system for the generation which should find the wit to resolve the conflicts he had pointed out, went slowly out of life, lonely, trivial, unappeased and disagreeable. But that was probably all in the character he had chosen out of those available to him. He had acted a part until he was unable to discover his own nature. He had amused himself that way among his students—too long, for a man cannot act for himself alone, and he is sure to regret, if he lives to be old, and his associates fall away, that no one loves fiercely the bare bones of his body and spirit. At least there are plenty of signs that Veblen had such regret.

# VI.

# Dewey and His "Studies in Logical Theory"

## By C. E. AYRES

JOHN DEWEY was born on October 20, 1859, in Burlington, Vermont. He was educated in the local schools and at the University of Vermont, from which he received his bachelor's degree in 1879. After taking his Ph.D. at Johns Hopkins in 1884, he taught successively at the University of Minnesota (1885–89), the University of Michigan (1889–94), the University of Chicago (1894–1904), where he was also director of the School of Education, and Columbia University, where he has remained. During leaves of absence he has traveled widely and lectured in cities all over the world—Peking, Tokyo, Paris, Constantinople, Moscow, Edinburgh.

In Chicago Dr. Dewey was one of the first members of the board of trustees at Hull House. Since then he has taken an active interest in social welfare and political reform movements. He has served at the head of such different organizations as the League for Independent Political Action, the American Association of University Professors, the American Philosophical Association and the committee of inquiry into the charges against Leon Trotsky. His real influence, however, has been exerted not in politics but in the two fields of philosophy and education.

In philosophy he has developed the system known as Instrumentalism, by his writings on logic, epistemology, psychology, ethics and esthetics. In education not only has he written widely —attacking authoritarian methods and defending the ideal of learning through experimentation and practice—but he also founded an experimental high school that served as a model for scores of others, and has seen his methods partly adopted by American school boards and foreign governments. Among his books are "Psychology" (1887), "The School and Society" (1889), "Ethics" (with James H. Tufts, 1908), "Democracy and Education" (1916), "Human Nature and Conduct" (1922), "Experience and Nature" (1925), "The Quest for Certainty" (1929) and "Art as Experience" (1934).

A<small>T THE AGE OF SEVENTY-NINE</small>
John Dewey published a treatise on logic. This event,
sufficiently remarkable in itself, was a joke of Olympian proportions on the world of 1938.

Dewey was at the apex of his reputation in the twenties. Wilsonian idealism and the war gave national
scope to the leadership he had attained in education
and philosophy by the publication of "Democracy and
Education" and the "Essays in Experimental Logic,"
both in 1916. In the hush of normalcy his voice was
more audible than ever. No American, not even Emerson, has ever been more widely and fully acknowledged
as the intellectual leader of the nation than was Dewey
at that time. When the Carus lectureship was established to be a forum for the maturest expression of our
philosophic minds, it was assumed as a matter of course
that Dewey should be the first Carus lecturer; and a
few years later he followed Josiah Royce and William
James (after an interval of more than a quarter of a

century) to the Gifford lectureship at Edinburgh, historically perhaps the loftiest philosophic platform in the world. These lectures, published as "Experience and Nature" and "The Quest for Certainty," were hailed as Dewey's consummate achievement.

But that was not the end either of Dewey or the world. Much has happened in the last ten years. The loving veneration which Dewey's name aroused only a few years ago has become clouded with a faint sense of fatigue and even of impatience. I suppose this was inevitable. Veneration is a fatiguing exercise, and in the course of years Dewey's ideas have become commonplace. The younger generation was born speaking Dewey's language. To them it is their language, not his. They get no thrills from his recent books because his earlier books had become the stuff of their own thoughts, while to the older generation his latest treatise, "Logic: the Theory of Inquiry," "contains nothing new." It is a very hefty job, we all agree, "the clearest and much the most complete statement he has made of his logical position, a very creditable performance indeed and truly astonishing for a man of his age; but the point of view is substantially that of his 'Studies in Logical Theory,' contributed to the Decennial Publications of the University of Chicago in 1903."

In those "Studies" the whole force of the attack was directed against Lotze. This point is one of considerable moment. Lotze is no more than Hecuba to the present generation, but that only goes to show how different the world is now from what it was when the ideas for which Dewey stands were first enunciated. We have indeed grown up. To what extent we owe our maturity to the individual influence of John Dewey, who can say? We have no yardstick for measuring the quantity of intellectual influence. But qualities are more amenable to understanding. The character of Dewey's influence, certainly, is clear and definite. It can be adequately expressed, I think, only in terms of the commonplace and its opposite, the occult, conceived as a pervading quality not merely of the weird beliefs of remote savages but of the "common sense," as Veblen put it, of the most highly civilized communities.

Our civilization is in process of emerging from the occult on a grand scale. Some readers may be tempted to dismiss this characterization as a merely rhetorical overstatement. It is not intended as such. It is not even meant as a reproach. Our past leaves no ground for such reproaches. The truth is that even in the twentieth century we are only men and the recent descendants of savages. All that we ordinarily think of as civilization has come about within a hundred generations or so, and these hundred generations were preceded by a period at least ten times as long, perhaps a hundred times, of utter, abject, groveling obsession with the occult. That we should be haunted by such a past is inevitable under the circumstances.

Furthermore, we are not omniscient even today. Science has revealed a little something of the movements of the stars and the electrons, we know a little something about the circulation of the blood and a tiny bit about the central nervous system; but beyond this smattering on all sides lies the vasty deep of the unknown, still the natural habitat of Awful Powers. To be sure, we might argue that whenever science does penetrate the unknown the newly discovered territory always turns out to be exactly like our own backyard.

But for some reason we never do. That takes genius, Dewey's kind of genius, a special affinity for the commonplace. Most people are still sure, in spite of a thousand contrary demonstrations, that Mystery lies just beyond the latest scientific fence.

For example, there is Beauty—with a capital B. People who scoff at talk of the occult are (perhaps for that reason) the very ones to insist on spelling it that way. Beauty, they insist, is Something Apart. They find it hard to say just what distinguishes the beautiful from the commonplace. Indeed they dismiss the attempt as itself commonplace: trying to apply common, vulgar word-haggling to what is Unique, Transcendent, a quality of the Spirit that only can be known intuitively and only by the finer spirits, those who are in tune with the Infinite. Minus the sarcasm, that is how they put it. But to a vulgar reasoner, what they are in tune with is capital letters; that is, with arbitrary and absolute distinctions, that is, with the occult.

The beautiful is of course a member of a celebrated triad, and as such partakes of the nature of the true and the good—or the other way around. I have led the ace of esthetics in the hope that it would take a trick. For various reasons it is easier for most people to spot hocus-pocus in High Art than in matters which are their own daily concern. But the same occultism pervades status and authority of every kind. By whatever means an oil company manages to wangle a concession, the rights they have acquired forthwith become Property with a capital P, as sacred and indissoluble as the Fundamentalist conception of the marriage tie; and any later proposal to modify, let alone dissolve, those rights will excite in the breasts of the devout the same horror with which good Catholics contemplate divorce.

There is no restricted zone to which the occult is confined. It trickles down the ages and oozes imperceptibly from one regime to its successor. For example, note the irony of John Locke's classic formulation of the theory of property. Locke denounced the humbug of the divine right of kings, to which for good measure he opposed the right of property; and to make his case unbeatable he endowed property with all the sacred attributes he had just stripped from royalty, even including divine origin. Curiously enough we have done the same thing with democracy. Instead of dispensing with the idea of sovereignty we have carefully retained the ancient myth, merely transferring its prerogative from kings to the Sovereign People. Thus it comes about that even in the twentieth century many people still imagine that Democracy—with a capital D, like Property and Beauty—is a sort of sacred flame which might be instantaneously extinguished by any coup d'état and can therefore be kept alight only by the violent suppression of undemocratic enterprises.

## II

If we are emerging from the occult, it is by a process altogether different from the substitution of one political regime for another political regime or of one set of rights for another set of rights with different beneficiaries but the same content of traditional beliefs. In this sense democracy is not the Rule of the People but the growth of enlightenment. Dewey has always identified it with education, not in the sense of government by professors but with the idea, apparently, that understanding is more important than authority. What makes the devices of suffrage and representation important, and what makes them work in so far as they do work, is general literacy, the growth of the informed interest of people generally in their general as well as individual concerns.

Obviously this educational process far transcends the schools. Modern enlightenment stems from science, from discovery and invention, from the elaboration of all the useful arts of which science is the rationale. The invention of printing has had something to do with it. So has the expansion of the material culture of the whole industrial community by virtue of which great masses of people have been lifted out of the physical and emotional importunacy of squalor and unremitting drudgery. So has the infiltration of highly technical skills. Which has been the greatest educator, Henry Ford or Lee De Forest, Model T's or audion tubes?

Doubtless schools also have something to do with the educational process. Since schools must have teachers, and since teachers must have something to teach, the schools have become the chief patrons of discovery and invention, the advancement of science and the arts; and with the increasing elaboration of our scientific culture the schools have become increasingly important as the medium of diffusion of skills and of ideas. It is therefore quite appropriate that a man of Dewey's stripe should be thought of as an educator. Probably no other individual has ever exerted more influence on American education than John Dewey. Nevertheless, the force of his personal impact on education, as on modern thought, derives from the fact that it is more than personal. It is the influence not of a man but of an idea and a process, and it can be understood only by grasping that idea.

The keynote of modern education is its continuity with life. We must never forget that when education was made universal (almost within the memory of living men) the tradition it was called upon to universalize was that of class education. Tom Brown's father sent him off to Rugby with instructions to become an English gentleman whether or not he mastered Greek, but of course with the conviction that mastering Greek in childhood was the way to become an English gentleman. Education meant Culture with a capital C, standing also for Class. Modern schools are still struggling with that tradition: struggling to make the content of the teaching continuous with the content of modern life by insinuating into the curriculum first science and then social studies; struggling to give the pupils' schooling some continuity with their own actual life, present and future; struggling to release individual abilities on the cultivation of which the future of democracy depends from the regimentation required by Father Brown and his Class.

It is a difficult and dangerous job. Who knows what education is of the most worth? Take mathematics, for example. At least 99 percent of all the mathematics taught in colleges and secondary schools today is a sheer waste of effort, and yet mathematics is beyond question one of the most important factors of modern civilization. It is easy enough to make education relevant to life by confining the education of the masses to teaching them a trade, but is that education or serfdom? Conceived as Dewey has always understood it, education is a phase of the larger process of the realization of democracy and the emergence of the modern mind from immemorial tradition, a process by virtue of which our schools have become more truly a cross-section of American culture (small c) and more effectively a part of American life as a whole than schools have ever been before.

To credit such a movement to an individual would be fantastic. But even glaciers have their contours; and this process, general as it is, nevertheless turns upon an idea as specific as that of the origin of species and one quite as definitely attributable to Dewey as evolution to Charles Darwin. In a general way modern enlightenment is a function of science. But as we have already noted, even science has its boundaries, some say limitations. What lies beyond those boundaries? Shall we be scientific as far as science goes, and beyond that point reaffirm the ancient traditions of our race? Must we do so? Are we by nature dual personalities, the schizophrenic creatures of a bifurcated world? This is a philosophic question, and it is the answer he proposed as a philosopher that is the source of all John Dewey's influence.

### III

As a philosopher Dewey has been concerned with the true, the good and the beautiful, that is to say with meanings and values; and the values are contingent on the meanings. "Art as Experience," the William James lectures given at Harvard University after his retirement from active service at Columbia, is the most successful attempt anyone has ever made to treat the experience of beauty as an integral and active part of our common life. "Human Nature and Conduct," in which he did the same for morals, has achieved the status of a classic by inclusion in the Modern Library. But the beautiful and the good derive from the true. If art and morality are continuous with the whole of life, the essential continuity is that of thought. That idea is the source from which all Dewey's many and various interpretations flow. Given his "Studies in Logical Theory," somebody else might have done "Art as Experience," as after a fashion several people have; but the reverse would have been impossible.

The reason is that Dewey's logic is focused on the axioms, postulates or preconceptions on which all our thinking builds. Our deepest divisions of opinion develop from our preconceptions. As Clarence Day once wrote, it makes all the difference in the world whether we are super-apes or fallen angels. This difference of assumption with which two groups of students face their facts has sometimes been referred to Darwinism and sometimes to behaviorism, and both are germane here. Why has Darwinism cut so deeply through the whole of modern thought? Why should Dewey's colleague, Veblen, have dismissed classical economic theory precisely on the ground that it is pre-Darwinian? Why should Dewey have written an essay on the influence of Darwinism on philosophy and then have thought that early essay sufficiently important to give its title to his first volume of collected papers? Not, I think, because Darwinism means change or even development. Outraged conservatives have always protested vehemently that economics dealt with change long before Darwin, and they are right. The real difference is in what is conceived to change. Darwin made the human species continuous with other species and therefore an organism, continuous with all protoplasm, and so with molecules and atoms, geologic strata and stellar galaxies. With evolution science annexed mankind. Beyond science lies the unknown, but man is no longer a part of it. To a Darwinian the idea that man can know himself only by inner contemplation is abyssal nonsense—and all that follows from it.

The issue of behaviorism runs to the same effect. This word has become intensely unpopular among psychologists because it has been claimed as the all-but-registered trademark of a narrow clique. The profession generally resents the pretensions of this clique, its claims to priority and its attempt to dictate the terms and methods by use of which alone psychology may be a science. As every student knows, behaviorism was preceded by functionalism; and as to introspection, which the behaviorist fraternity condemns so utterly, there is no valid reason why a psychologist should not use himself as a subject for experimentation any more than a physiologist, provided he is not making self-observation the pretext for assuming that one's self is a window through which to peer mysteriously inward at the Soul. And no psychologist does this any more. In America at least all modern psychology is behaviorism in the larger sense of the study of the behavior of the human (social) animal. As a science psychology has abandoned the occult much more generally than economics.

This whole movement flows directly from Dewey's instrumental logic. Perhaps we should not attach too much importance to merely personal incidents, but it is worth noting by the way that the leaders of both the behaviorist and the functionalist schools began their studies under Dewey. Certainly their conclusions flowed from his assumptions. In the preface to the 1916 edition of his "Essays in Experimental Logic," Dewey remarked that the perspicacious reader would see in them the groundwork of what had since come to be known as behaviorism; and in the 1903 edition of the earlier studies he noted that "this point of view makes it possible for logical theory to come to terms with psychology," with a cross-reference to Angell's essay on functional psychology in the same Chicago decennial series.

IV

The point of view of Instrumentalism (or pragmatism as William James had called it) can be understood only in contrast to the immemorial tradition it opposed. Traditional logic had always regarded truth as an inherent quality of thought. From Aristotle to the mathematical logicians of today, its concern has been with internal consistency, the purely formal relationships of a series of ideas or propositions. Thus "All men are mortal; Socrates is a man; therefore Socrates is mortal," is said to be a sound bit of reasoning because the formal relationships between major premise, minor premise and conclusion are all according to Hoyle. But can we discuss the truth of a proposition until we know what it means? And can we begin to know what it means until we know who is saying it and why, what difference its assertion makes to what situation? The drift of these questions has often been misrepresented by stupid and unscrupulous critics. As they would have it, Instrumentalism (or pragmatism

as they usually prefer to call it, because the rash elo-
quence of William James more often drops its guard)
amounts to saying that an idea is true if it works. For
example, the Nazi theory of race is true since it has
served to regenerate the German people. It ought not
to be necessary to deny that Dewey ever said or that
James ever meant anything like that. What they might
have said is that the Nazi theory of race is neither a
scientific truth nor a scientific error; it is pure nonsense
knowingly employed for purposes of political suasion,
and as such its scientific and logical significance is the
same as that of Shelley's statement that the skylark is
not a bird. In each case the use to which the proposition is put, that is, its instrumentality, determines what
it means, and that meaning determines what we are
to think of it and do about it logically and scientifically.

The issue of course goes much deeper than academic
logic-chopping—that is why old traditions have been so
persistent and modern conservatism so bitterly recal-
citrant. Truth has been regarded as an inherent quality
of thought because to a certain type of mind thought
itself has always seemed to be the ultimate reality.
Thus our conception of values, social, moral and esthetic, turns on our notion of mind; and our conception
of mind turns on our notion of the thought process.
Does the thought process itself inwardly reveal a
mysterious universe of spirit that lies beyond the reach
of scientific instruments? That is what savages believe,
and after them theologians, and after them metaphysi-
cians. I think; therefore my thought is pure Idea and my
mind pure Spirit. It was that tradition which Dewey
confronted in the contemporary of his younger days,
Lotze. He confronted it with the basic scientific princi-

ple of continuity and with a philosophically calculated
naïveté:

> Thinking is a kind of activity which we perform at specific
> need, just as at other need we engage in other sorts of activity.
> . . . The measure of its success, the standard of its validity,
> is precisely the degree in which thinking actually disposes of the
> difficulty and allows us to proceed with the more direct modes
> of experiencing, that are forthwith possessed of more assured
> and deepened value.

Thus he closed the abyss between thought and things,
on the brink of which generation after generation of
philosophers had mulled and mumbled, by a declaration as simple and direct as that of the urchin in the
presence of the naked king: that no such cleft exists or
ever existed:

> This point of view knows no fixed distinction between the
> empirical values of unreflective life and the most abstract proc-
> ess of rational thought. It knows no fixed gulf between the
> highest flight of theory and control of the details of practical
> construction and behavior. It passes, according to the occasion
> and opportunity of the moment, from the attitude of loving
> and struggling and doing to that of thinking and the reverse.
> Its contents or material shift their values back and forth from
> technological or utilitarian to esthetic, ethic or affectional. . . .
> In all this there is no difference of kind between the methods
> of science and those of the plain man. . . . The fundamental
> assumption is *continuity* in and of experience.

In these sentences, published in 1903, I believe that
future historians will find an essential clue to the turn
civilization has taken in our time and to the relation
of John Dewey to that movement. Consequently I regard "Studies in Logical Theory" as the more important book for the student of Dewey's mind and in-

fluence, as I think most students do. But I should not advise a student of the contemporary world to read it. For one thing, it has been out of print for years. Then too the shade of Lotze hovering in the background is distracting even to readers who do not believe in ghosts. The late reader should read the latest book. If he will raise the cover of "Logic: the Theory of Inquiry," he will find that the author begins his preface by declaring that "this book is a development" of the earlier "Studies" and "Essays," and then proceeds at once to call attention "to the principle of the continuum of inquiry, a principle whose importance, so far as I am aware, only Peirce had previously noted." The book itself is Dewey's definitive exposition of just what it means to say that human thought is a process that occurs in nature, what it means for the theory of knowledge, for the conventions of logical analysis, for science and its laws and finally for social inquiry.

**v**

It will be interesting to see what our world does with such a book. For we live in a strange world. With more knowledge, more skill, more tools at our command than men have ever had, we seem to be losing faith in knowledge, skill and tools and reverting to passion and mythology. I have ascribed the dwindling of Dewey's fame to the growing familiarity of his ideas, but obviously that is only part of the story. Mr. Earl Browder is said to have defined a liberal as one who raises doubt and indecision to the level of a principle. This is a splendid definition. It states the opposite principle of violence most clearly and succinctly. By contriving to avoid all encumbering questions as to what the violence is for, it makes that principle equally congenial to all direct-actionists, whether communist or fascist; and by making liberalism the alternative to all this it achieves a clarity which could scarcely be improved upon. Nothing defines the scientific state of mind better than doubt, and the democratic principle is precisely that of solving problems not by "decisive" authority but with understanding and the slow but eventually sure seepage of ideas through the whole community. John Dewey is a liberal in this sense; and in so far as the influence of these ideas is really waning in favor of the principle of meeting force with "decisive" force, Dewey's influence is really waning.

At the University of Chicago, where Dewey's ideas were the paramount influence for about three decades, a revolt has been going on. I am told that it is leading toward a sort of "neo-Thomism." Advanced Marxians also find Dewey unsatisfactory. These are signs of the times. I have read only one review of "Logic: the Theory of Inquiry," but I note with interest that the reviewer finds "that there remain unanswered certain fundamental questions which have troubled those who find Instrumentalism . . . inconclusive." I have no reason to suppose that the reviewer is a member either of the Thomist or the Marxian communion, but his state of mind is perhaps revealed by the ensuing question: "May there not be some basic reason in the very nature of things for the fact that one idea or way of acting proves successful when put into operation, while another does not?" To the innocent readers such a question may seem innocent and even reasonable. But these Fundamental Questions about Basic Reasons for the

Very Nature of Things: do they really appeal to the intelligence, or to the sense of propriety? Before the reader decides, perhaps he would do well to read "The Quest for Certainty." It is not an accident that every dogma has its hierarchy and every totalitarian regime its dogma; and it is not by omission that Dewey fails to provide us with a dogma or a dialectic. His influence flows in precisely the opposite direction. Whether the ideas he stands for will prevail—who knows? But nobody need be in any doubt as to what they are. They are the art of thinking and living in the lower case. In the bedlam of tragedy, melodrama and light opera in which we live, Dewey is still the master of the commonplace.

# VII.

# Boas and "The Mind of Primitive Man"

## By PAUL RADIN

FRANZ BOAS was born on July 9, 1858, in Minden, Germany. He studied at Heidelberg, Bonn and Kiel, receiving his doctorate from the last of these universities in 1881. He taught geography at the University of Berlin in 1885–86 and at the same time was assistant in the Royal Ethnographic Museum. In 1888 he came to Clark University in Worcester, Massachusetts; in 1892–95 he was chief assistant in the Department of Anthropology at the Chicago World's Fair. Boas was one of the first anthropologists to spend much time in the field, making expeditions to Baffin Island (1883 and 1886), to Mexico, Puerto Rico and elsewhere. He has devoted a whole series of monographs to the Kwakiutl Indians of British Columbia. He has also been a pioneer in the statistical analysis of human measurements and in studying the effect of environmental conditions on race physique and the results of racial crossing. From 1901 to 1905 he was curator of anthropology at the American Museum of Natural History.

Before this time, in 1899, he had been named the first professor of anthropology at Columbia University. Under his direction, the Columbia Department of Anthropology became internationally famous. There he trained a whole generation of anthropologists who are now applying his methods, especially to the study of the American Indians, the South Sea Islanders and the African Negroes. There is scarcely an American university where his influence has not been felt. Boas retired from active teaching in 1937 and now bears the title of professor emeritus in residence. His most important works since "The Mind of Primitive Man" are "Primitive Art" (1927) and "Anthropology and Modern Life" (1928). The fine article on anthropology which he contributed to the Encyclopedia of the Social Sciences states his theories in brief.

THE TASK OF AN EVALUATOR is at
all times beset with difficulties. It is a thankless one at
best, for he must always be prepared to meet the ac-
cusation that, in some unexplained manner, he is largely
responsible for the condition to which he calls attention. This is particularly true when it is a question of
evaluating any work that deals with the analysis and
history of society.

We would all agree today that a man's basic conditioning is nowhere more obvious than when he is
dealing with the history of his fellow men and when he
attempts to describe and find reasons for their activities.

A generation ago this did not seem so apparent, and
many who concerned themselves with the social sciences
regarded scientific objectivity as something self-evident,
a state of mind that all rigorously trained thinkers
acquired automatically by an honest contemplation of
the facts and by hard and painstaking work. They took
their task sternly, armed with what Franz Boas himself has suggestively termed a "cold enthusiasm for
the truth." The making of an accurate record de-

pended, they felt, not so much upon the observer or any special insight he possessed as upon the recognition of the true physiognomy that social facts assumed. These facts were always present and constituted discrete and objective realities. All they demanded was to be given their own autonomy and to be properly arranged.

This was admittedly no easy task, for not only did it require a long preparation and apprenticeship, but facts did not take kindly to everyone. The obverse, that a special temperament or social-political conditioning might actually constrain them to take a somewhat willful attitude toward the facts, never occurred as a possibility. Besides, one could rely upon the facts taking care of themselves and guarding their own integrity.

When Boas's "Mind of Primitive Man" appeared in 1911, so completely was the possibility of scientific objectivity accepted as an axiom, and so safe appeared to be the foundations of the society in which he lived, that only surprise and a kindly bewilderment greeted what he set before the American public. Yet he had formulated something of a revolutionary thesis and, properly speaking, the world should have been shaken to its innermost core. If the data which he presented were accurate, then all the accepted and cherished correlations that had been established between the various aspects of our civilization, not to mention many of our accepted values, had no inherent justification. If he was right, no guarantee existed that they would persist. Indeed, reasons were advanced to show that they were iniquitous to the heart, insulting to the mind, and ought not to persist.

What Boas made clear was that an "objective"

study of the aboriginal populations of the world, as well as the activities and ideas developed in connection with them—a study freed from the obvious distortions introduced by observers who had certain theses to support—played havoc with the basic correlations accepted as proved by contemporary opinion. He demonstrated conclusively that races and sub-races were mixed and possessed no stability; that no language was, in any meaningful sense, superior to another or better capable of expressing ideas than another, and that no connection existed between the physical type of a given population, its language and the culture it developed.

He contended more specifically that a given race attains civilization because of particular historical events and not because of any particular faculty—today we would say inherent traits—it possesses. Consequently it is entirely erroneous to assume that one race is more highly gifted than another. He showed conclusively, to use his own words, that "the average faculty of the white race is found to the same degree in a large proportion of individuals of all other races . . . and that there is no reason to suppose that they are unable to reach the level of civilization represented by the bulk of our own people." He also attacked the superficial impression held by so many people, educated as well as uneducated, that any correlation exists between distinct languages, distinct cultures and distinct racial types. It was exceedingly easy for him to demonstrate that a change in culture may exist with constancy in physical type and language; that language may change and physical type remain constant or that, finally, language may remain constant and physical type and culture alter profoundly.

The implications were plain. The explanation of differences in custom and belief was not to be sought in the language people spoke, or the physical type they possessed, but in the way in which they combined and arranged the data at their disposal. These arrangements and correlations were as valid as our own. That so much appears strange and irrational to us in the world of primitive men is due to our inability to shake off the influences of the traditional culture in which we have been reared. If their cultures seem on the whole inadequate, that can easily be accounted for. The accumulated knowledge on which they depend is not only quantitatively smaller, but is entangled in emotional adhesions that are qualitatively much stronger than those existing among ourselves. It is this existence of multiple types of society, Boas contended, that we must learn to recognize, as well as the dangers inhering in any attempt to evaluate them ethically or arrange them historically.

Such, in brief, was the argument of "The Mind of Primitive Man." That it should have had little immediate effect on his contemporaries, outside the circle of his students and professional colleagues, is easily understood. How could ordinary people accept the idea that there is no inherent connection between race and culture, or admit that inflectional languages, like the Indo-European and the Semitic, should be put on a par with the agglutinative and polysynthetic idioms of American and African aborigines? Even scholars were slow to accept Boas's theories, though his influence was spreading. As late as the 1920's, a Cambridge professor could still maintain that the Greek translation of Goethe's "Über allen Gipfeln ist Ruh" was superior to the original German because Greek was, after all, the more mature language. A distinguished archeologist could insist that the Nordic superiority in physique fitted its possessors to become the vehicles of a superior language. Of course still greater nonsense has been spoken and written since 1933, but that is in Germany, a country where scientific anthropology has been abolished.

When "The Mind of Primitive Man" was revised and reissued in 1938, Boas added a fine chapter on "The Race Problem in Modern Society." It is his answer both to Hitler and to those of our own countrymen who argue that Negroes are incapable of achieving a high civilization.

II

Although the world at large was impervious to Boas's message when it was first delivered, the students of American ethnology were not. To them, his theories meant a liberation from subjective evaluations and antiquated methods of approach. The essence of his method was, as we have seen, to gather facts and ever more facts—ethnological, linguistic, anatomical—in the most careful manner possible, and to let the facts speak for themselves, irrespective of the conclusions to which they led. There was to be no shrinking from these conclusions even if they meant that cherished and generally accepted classifications and syntheses were proved to be inaccurate.

All this was like a breath of fresh air. If the emphasis was placed fairly exclusively on the obtaining of a proper record, and if a synthesis was eschewed for analysis, that seemed not only excusable but even justifiable. Under Boas's stimulation ethnologists set to work to describe the facts "as they really were," to make no judgments and scrupulously to avoid not only generalizations but also any attempt at arranging the facts in a historical sequence.

Yet to one aspect of his work American ethnologists remained singularly unresponsive in any concrete way, namely, its practical implications. To them "The Mind of Primitive Man" enunciated a new methodology to be used in obtaining and understanding ethnological data. By implication they felt that it discouraged any active participation in the affairs of the world. The only legitimate method of changing the attitude of people toward such questions as race or cultural achievements, they contended, was to present them with the facts. To force them to act upon these facts was not only outside the proper domain of the scientist and scholar—who were, after all, simply fact-finders—but definitely an infraction of their main thesis, that all points of view have a right to self-expression.

They were entirely justified in regarding this attitude as an integral element in the argument of "The Mind of Primitive Man." We are definitely told there that the hereditary mental faculty has probably not been improved by civilization and that, in the transition from primitive to civilized society, the only changes occurring have been the decrease in the number of emotional associations and the improvement of the traditional material that enters into our mental operations.

At first blush this sounds almost like a doctrine of quietism. As a matter of fact it did lead, in some cases, if not to quietism, at least to a spirited defense of tra-

ditionalism and traditional institutions. For instance,
one of Boas's former students, Lowie, is willing to ascribe the arrested progress of the physical sciences
during the Middle Ages to the spontaneous human
adherence to tradition rather than to the external pressure of a hostile church, and to state that "an unbiased
view of human history leads to a revision of the received rationalist program of future progress." To
such an amazingly complacent justification of the accepted order of things could the fundamental thesis of
Boas's book be transformed.

Now it may strike us as somewhat incredible that a
point of view ostensibly so liberating as that of Boas's
could lead to a defense of traditionalism. Yet this can
be said to flow directly from the fundamental presuppositions that lay concealed in Boas's methods of approach and interpretation of the data. To understand
why this was so, we must, however, first try to de-
termine the nature of his conception of the relations
of the individual to the group as well as his explanation
of the causes for social stability and change.

### III

For Boas the only true conditioning factors in culture are the biological and the ideological. From the
first, an individual derives his physical and mental-
emotional make-up; from the second, the specific content of his mind. Both are imposed from without.
Freedom of individual action is, under these conditions,
impossible except for individuals who are willing to
brave the dangers that attend any marked deviation
from tradition and who are by that very fact to be

regarded as pathological. The role of the individual is thus reduced entirely to one of personal relationships. He is of value only as illustration. Thus for Boas, and for all those who remained loyal to his point of view—the majority often did so without their being aware of it—society was an entity in itself, although carried by men and existing through them.

From such an attitude there flowed, inevitably, certain stresses and specific interests. The study of the individual was interpreted as belonging within the domain of psychology. Indeed, with some of Boas's later students, it has been signed over to the psychiatrist and psychoanalyst. The anthropologist was to deal only with the depiction and analysis of conditions and processes. He had nothing to do with the agencies producing the conditions or operative in the processes.

This was naturally a somewhat difficult position to maintain. Yet, in so far as possible, Boas maintained it. For example, he insisted that while, in the development of civilization, our logical processes tend to eliminate traditional elements, no marked decrease has taken place in the force of those traditional elements contained in our activities. These are and must be exclusively controlled by custom. This view he reiterates in the new edition of "The Mind of Primitive Man": "The dynamic forces that mold social life are the same now as those that molded life thousands of years ago."

In the light of what has just been pointed out, his approach to the problem of social stability and change is not difficult to understand. Stability exists wherever activities are strongly surcharged with emotional associations, and change takes place whenever the majority of cultural activities have not entered deeply enough into the mind to give them emotional values.

This is indeed a foolproof ideological heaven. It was not created by Boas, but is the work of his teacher and master, Adolf Bastian. To the latter's theory of "elementary ideas," elementary ideas which develop with iron necessity wherever man lives, Boas has always remained faithful. A clear enunciation of these elementary ideas, so Boas assures us, will give us the psychological reasons for their existence. Man, in short, is mired in conditions over which he has no control and shackled to inexorable categories of the mind from which he can never be freed. At best he can only hope to reshuffle and recombine, possibly to refine them.

Boas's approach to the data of ethnology thus contained postulates that belonged to a fairly closed metaphysical system. The novelty and the liberating quality of his approach to cultural data did not lie in any of its presuppositions. These patently hark back to the neo-Kantian tradition in which all German scholars of the second half of the nineteenth century had been reared. It lay, rather, in the fact that such a point of view had never before been rigorously applied to the elucidation of aboriginal cultures, and in the circumstance that its application enabled ethnologists to develop a proper appreciation for cultural pluralism and cultural relativity.

This was no small achievement and should, in its turn, have led to a fundamental renovation of the social sciences, particularly of history. Yet it did not do so. It was no accident that, on the contrary, it encouraged a militant antagonism to historical reconstructions and syntheses. All its postulates, its whole methodology, were based on assumptions which not only excluded the recognition of the developmental sequences that are the lifeblood of the social sciences, but actually brought about the omission of the facts that would have made it possible for such sequences and correlations to have been established. In other words, the chosen approach dictated what data were to be selected. And this was all the more dangerous because no one seemed to be aware of it.

The implications that flowed from these postulates are nowhere better illustrated than by the finality with which Boas and his school rejected the evolutionary societal progressions proposed by the English anthropological theorists and the American, Lewis Morgan. To have pointed out the errors, the inadequacies and the crudities contained in the various schematic societal sequences was one thing, and for this the world can only thank them. However, to have rejected the possibility and the necessity for establishing such sequences implied a complete misunderstanding by Boas and his school of the actual nature of social facts, and deprived those facts of all their reality. This was a danger which the great legal historian Maitland had sensed when he insisted that anthropology would eventually have to make the choice between becoming history or nothing. Boas's point of view in this regard meant that the civilizations of primitive peoples were never to be properly understood, and their relation to our own never appreciated. Furthermore it entailed an obvious distortion of the factual record and actually nullified, in part, the vital inferences drawn as to race, language and culture. Anthropology as cultivated in the United States was henceforth to operate in a vacuum. Its liberating messages, scientific and practical, were to be stillborn.

Boas could talk as courageously as he wished about there being no pure races and say that no specific mental and emotional traits had ever been connected with particular races or with particular cultures. The whole force of his findings was neutralized by the fact that his method of approach prevented him from understanding when it was that peoples had first begun to preach the doctrine of social and cultural superiority, and why. Similarly he and his students could insist as vehemently as they might that no connection existed between the economic and political structure of primitive civilizations, on the one hand, and their ideas and general intellectual achievements on the other. This ran so obviously counter to all that was true in the history of our own cultures that little credence was placed in their pronouncements. Something fundamentally erroneous, it was suspected, must inhere in a method that led to such sterility.

These suspicions were only too justified. The approach to social facts first developed in "The Mind of Primitive Man" was and always remained a purely philosophical-psychological one, and this in the sense of the German psychology of the latter part of the nineteenth century. The fundamental premises of Boas and his school made it necessary for them to deny the existence of the whole historical process, in the ordinary sense of that term.

It is, for instance, no mere accident that induces Boas to say in the 1938 edition of his book that "from a psychological point of view there is nothing that would help us to establish a time sequence for agriculture and herding." Nor is it a confusion of mind that induces one of his later students to insist that the synthesis apparent in a ritual is due to the prevalence of a specific style of religious behavior common to all the individuals in the tribe and not to historic causes. Nor is it strange that psychoanalysis is being welcomed today by so many of Boas's disciples. Psychoanalysis, on its theoretical side, is closely allied with many of the psychological principles enunciated by Boas.

Even more fateful than this anti-historical bias was the influence Boas exerted in preventing the recognition of certain facts, his denial of connections that should be patent to all students of history. When, for instance, he states that the simplest forms of the family are not associated with the simplest types of culture, that economic life and family organization are not intimately related or, finally, that "starvation among most primitive peoples is an exceptional case, the same as financial crises in civilized society; for times of need, such as occur regularly, provision is always made," what are we to think? For a person of Boas's integrity and scientific caution to have made such statements requires explanation. The explanation is close at hand. It lies in the curious omission from all his publications of the role played by economic factors in history.

IV

Of the great intellectual events of Boas's lifetime, assuredly the two most significant were the theory of evolution and the materialistic interpretation of history. To the first Boas always took a prevailingly antagonistic position, in so far as it threatened to influence his own branch of science. The second he never so much as mentioned until the 1938 edition of "The Mind of Primitive Man." There he dismisses it in a paragraph. He so completely misunderstands it as to say that "cultural life is always economically conditioned and economics are always culturally conditioned." Marx and Engels are never referred to. He did, of course, take a definite position toward the work upon which Engels's "Origins of the Family" was based, namely, Morgan's "Primitive Society." But, as we know, he saw in that book simply a crude and unjustified attempt to discover evolutionary stages in the history of society. To all Boas's disciples Morgan has since remained anathema and unread.

In part we must unquestionably ascribe this neglect of the role of economics to his basic outlook and the methodology in which it was expressed. In part, too, we should remember that he was originally trained in geography and psychophysics. Yet this is, at best, only part of the explanation. Boas does, after all, belong to a specific class, namely, to the intellectual bourgeoisie of Germany that enjoyed such a magnificent efflorescence between 1880 and 1910. Whatever may have been its merits—and they were many—it owed its position, its freedom of expression within the realm of science and the great respect in which it was held, to the state that had been reared on the most efficient of the capitalist economies of the nineteenth century. The theoretical justification for this state was found in the critical idealism of Kant, in the categories of the mind and in the categorical imperative. In this philosophy the intellectual bourgeoisie had also been reared. Not only were the German professors unable to transcend

the ideas with which they had been so thoroughly in-
doctrinated; they had no inclination to question them
or to inquire too deeply either into the foundations of
the economic system to which they owed all their comfort, prestige and security, or into the conditions necessary for its stability.

The unwillingness to recognize historical progressions and stages, the failure to appreciate the materialistic interpretation of history, all this must be
attributed, in the final analysis, to the intellectual
atmosphere in which Boas was reared as well as to his
own social conditioning. I would be the last to under-
estimate the contributions made by the Germany of
1880–1910. But one great danger did lurk in its intellectual attitude, namely, that it tended to paralyze any
participation in the realm of action. Such paralysis
seems to afflict many anthropologists today in the presence of the fascist threats to civilization. If, fortu-
nately, it does not afflict all of them, that is because
wherever fascism exists and reaction prevails, anthropologists are suspect. Indeed, if any group of intellectuals should today be in the forefront of the battle
it is the anthropologists. Boas, of course, understands
this clearly, as his magnificent stand against fascism
demonstrates. Yet he and his disciples could contribute
more to this struggle if they would free themselves
once and for all from the ballast of neo-Kantian ideas
and middle-class attitudes which "The Mind of Primitive Man" unwittingly introduced into anthropology.

# VIII.

# Beard's "Economic Interpretation of the Constitution"

## By MAX LERNER

CHARLES AUSTIN BEARD was born in Knightstown, Indiana, on November 27, 1874. He was educated at De Pauw University, from which he was graduated in 1898, and at Oxford, Cornell and Columbia, receiving his Ph.D. from the last of these institutions in 1904. Columbia appointed him adjunct professor of politics in 1907 and soon afterwards made him a full professor. He held this post until 1917, when he resigned in protest against President Butler's denial of academic freedom in wartime.

He has never since held an academic position, yet his influence and prestige have steadily increased. For a time he was director of the Training School for Public Service in New York, then director of the Institute of Municipal Research in Tokyo, then advisor to Viscount Goto, Japanese Minister of Home Affairs, after the earthquake in 1923. In 1926 he was president of the American Political Science Association, and in 1933 president of the American Historical Association.

Meanwhile he has gone on writing—articles on political and economic questions and books on American and European history. With James Harvey Robinson he wrote a famous textbook, "The Development of Modern Europe" (1907). His "Economic Interpretation of the Constitution" was followed by "Economic Origins of Jeffersonian Democracy" (1915). In 1922 he published a defense of his method, "The Economic Basis of Politics." To the general public he is, of course, best known for his two-volume work, "The Rise of American Civilization," published in 1927. It was written with his wife, Mary R. Beard, as was his most recent work, "America in Mid-Passage," published in 1939.

A T COLUMBIA UNIVERSITY about a
quarter-century ago, crowded classrooms were listening
to an assistant professor in his late thirties expound
strange doctrine. His name was Charles A. Beard
and he was a tall rangy young man from Indiana, with
a sharp aquiline profile, looking half farmer and half
Roman philosopher. When he talked he threw back
his head and half-shut his eyes, but his doctrine was
such as to cause the ghosts of generations of Constitu-
tion-mongering professors to hover uneasily over his
classroom. The study of American history, he said, was
cluttered with myths that had more relevance to filial
piety than to the real past. He was concrete. Instead
of repeating Bancroft's sunny banalities on the guiding
hand of Providence in the affairs of the young Republic, which led to the conclusion that the Almighty must
have been a Federalist, he analyzed a batch of Treasury statistics, or dug up some pamphlets by John
Taylor. He was unafraid to incur the charge of ir-

reverence. He refused to convert his job into a pastorate for a herd of academic sacred cows.

Every great thinker stands between the dying and the being born, between old bones and new stirrings in the realm of thought. Beard in 1913 could see the disintegration of the filial historical school. In constitutional history the great names were still Bancroft, Schouler, Von Holst, Fiske and McLaughlin, but their authority had worn thin. By those in dominant tradition, American history was still written and taught with a mixture of formalist logic-chopping and the starspangled manner. But fresh work was getting done. Turner's frontier theory, first broached in 1893, represented an economic emphasis. In the year that Beard took his doctorate at Columbia, 1904, Thorstein Veblen at Chicago published his "Theory of Business Enterprise," which was to remake American economic thought. Among Beard's own colleagues at Columbia, a genuine intellectual renaissance was in process. John Dewey was making philosophy democratic and pragmatic, and James Harvey Robinson was extending the boundaries of history to include the whole realm of the history of ideas. But the strongest impulses were coming from the new jurisprudence. Holmes had struck in 1905 in his dissent in *Lochner v. N. Y.* the high pitch of American juristic thought. And in 1908, Louis Brandeis, the "People's Attorney" of Boston, had presented his famous *Müller v. Oregon* brief with two pages of legal argument and over a hundred pages of economic statistics—and had won the case. The same year that saw Beard's book on the Constitution published saw also Brooks Adams's "Theory of Social Revolution"—a merciless analysis of the Supreme

Court decisions and constitutional history from the standpoint of the historical materialism of an eccentric Bostonian aristocrat.

The fact is that Beard's book was no literary mutation. The intellectuals were writing in response to new movements for social justice—populism, trade-unionism, socialism, muckraking, the "new freedom," the "new nationalism." And these movements were themselves a response to the powerful compulsives of the new technology and the new system of class relations. Thus Beard's book was not so much influenced by Turner, Veblen, Holmes, Brandeis, Robinson, Wilson, T. R. and Brooks Adams as it was another outgrowth of the same social soil and intellectual climate. Beard was to write (with his wife) in his "Rise of American Civilization" in 1927 a Veblenian chapter on the intellectual history of this period:

Once the juristic wall was breached, a search began for the springs of motive that induced individuals and groups to take part in the governing process. . . . As fitted the machine age . . . the search for such origins opened a way into the realm of economic enterprise. When that departure was made, no sanctum could elude intruders; no department of government, legislative, executive or judicial, could avoid the light of scientific criticism.

Thus did the Beard of 1927 describe the forces that led the Beard of 1913 as an "intruder" into the "sanctum" of the economic motives of the Founding Fathers.

## II

The book that was the product of the intrusion was "An Economic Interpretation of the Constitution."

The title itself was enough to startle the academic and political tycoons: the very juxtaposition of our great Sacred Writing with so secular a phrase as "economic interpretation" conveyed to many the suggestion of outright blasphemy. And the book pulled few punches. It set out to explain the formation of the Constitution and the founding of the new government, not on the doctrinal plane of the "federal" as against "states' rights" doctrine, nor on the traditional plane of "compromises" between sections and between small and large states, but on the plane of economic interests.

The sheer masterful structure of the book has nowhere had adequate justice done to it. Beard must have had a premonition of the desperate resistance he would run into. He made his book a magnificently planned battle. He reconnoiters the enemy, surveys the ground, deploys his troops, opens fire, brings up his heaviest guns, and then systematically mops up and consolidates his position. Most great books require a creative act in the very summary of them. That is not true of Beard's. Its argument is patent for anyone who will take the trouble to read it, as so few have done. There is little in it of marginal suggestiveness—in fact, as literature that is its principal weakness. You get what the author is driving at in the very first chapter: after that, the interest of the book lies in seeing how he elaborates and defends his thesis. It is all a bit like a demonstration of a mathematical theorem. You feel like writing Q.E.D. at the end, or else "Not Proven." It is almost as if the author had set out with a deliberate severity to strip the book of every adornment, on the theory that a plain woman would be less suspected of being a wanton than an attractive one.

But if the manner is severe and geometrical, the matter must have been to the generation of 1913 brash and daring. Instead of proceeding with Bancroft on the hypothesis that American history had been determined by the "higher power" that operates in human affairs, or with the school of Herbert Adams and John Fiske on the hypothesis that the presiding power had been the genius of Teutonic tribal institutions, or with McMaster and Rhodes on the hypothesis that no hypothesis was necessary and that fact-gathering from archives and newspapers was enough, he proposed to proceed on "the theory of economic determinism"— which, he remarked, "has not been tried out in American history, and until it is tried out, it cannot be found wanting."

The book became thus an inquiry into the proposition that "the direct, impelling motive" in the formation and ratification of the Constitution "was the economic advantages which the beneficiaries expected would accrue to themselves first, from their action." To test this he set about making a survey of property interests in 1787, both in realty and personalty. It led to the hypothesis of an opposition of economic interest between the small farmers, the debtor class and the unpropertied urban dwellers on the one hand, and on the other the landed proprietors (Hudson Valley patroons and Southern slave-holders) and the groups with personalty interests (money loaned or seeking investment, state and Continental paper, manufacturing, shipping, trading and capital speculatively invested in Western lands). The interests of the propertied groups often clashed. But, whatever their differences, on one thing they were agreed: if they were to survive, then what was needed was a strong central government that would check radical state legislation, put down the open insurrections against property, create a unified tariff and monetary system and set up checks upon the action of the majority.

The political leaders of these propertied groups were compelled to resort to an extra-legal coup—a Constitutional Convention which adopted a revolutionary program and put it through in defiance of the provisions for amendment in the Articles of Confederation. The groups representing important personalty interests in the state legislatures quietly and carefully engineered the selection of their own delegates to the Convention. In the amazing Chapter V on "The Economic Interests of the Members of the Convention," which is the heart of the book, Beard examines in detail the economic interests and experience of each delegate and concludes that "not one member represented in his immediate personal economic interests the small farming or mechanic classes," while at least five-sixths (including the Convention's leaders) "were immediately, directly and personally interested in the outcome of their labors at Philadelphia, and were to a greater or less extent economic beneficiaries from the adoption of the Constitution." The document they constructed, for all that it was couched and defended in terms of political doctrine, was in all its implications and in its deepest meaning an economic document. The state ratifying conventions were chosen, because of property disqualifications or indifference, by a vote of not more than one-sixth of the adult males. They were certainly, in their leadership, representative of the same economic groups as the members of the original Conven-

tion. The whole process of ratifying this document had
the same aspects of a deliberately maneuvered coup by
the propertied interests as the calling of the Convention itself. Hamilton and Madison both justified their
procedure ultimately on the right of revolution, *i.e.,*
counter-revolution.

### III

One need scarcely say what an anguished cry arose
when the book appeared early in 1913, from the masters of property and their lieutenants in politics, in
law, in the press, in the academies and among the professional patrioteers. William Howard Taft and Elihu
Root both attacked it, and Taft, just become ex-Presi-
dent, not only mentioned it slightingly in his valedictory
book, "Popular Government," but went out of his way
to make a speech against it. A self-formed committee
of the New York Bar Association summoned Beard to
appear before it and defend his thesis: "and when I
declined . . ." Beard wrote later, "they treated my
reply as a kind of contempt of court." Some of the
reviewers showed a sense of injured national pride
amounting to hysteria. Albert Bushnell Hart, the
mogul of the historians, set the tone in his article,
"Baseless Slanders on Great Men." The Dial said of
the book that it "tends . . . to foster unjustified class
antagonism." J. H. Latane, in The American Political
Science Review, wrote, "It will require more convincing evidence . . . to upset the traditional view that
the members of the federal convention were patriotic
men earnestly striving to arrive at the best political
solution of the dangers that threatened the republic."
The Nation reviewed it rather favorably when it ap-

peared, but a year and a half later—perhaps when the editors had had a chance to digest the general hysteria —it published a scathing editorial called "Muckraking the Fathers." The Seattle high schools took the trouble to ban the book outright.

There were other and divergent voices. O. G. Libby, who had helped clear the ground on which Beard built, and William E. Dodd gave it courageous reviews. What happened in The New York Times was curious. It did not get a review at all for several months; then, on November 23, a week before the publication of the Times's list of the "100 Best Books of the Year" (chosen by an independent group of critics), there was a fair and cordial review: the next week it was one of the list. Parrington has written about Beard's thesis, in the third volume of his "Main Currents," that "the really surprising thing is that it should have come as a surprise." That would be true, if one could premise on the part of people a knowledge of what they ought to know if they were rational and sensible. Actually, given the way in which the book tore aside the veil of patriotism that clothed the role of big property in American history, the surprising thing is not that there was so much anguish when the book appeared, but that there was not more. That it was not unanimous testifies to the strength of the forces that had in the first instance brought the book to fruition.

What was maddening to those who raged against Beard was that he could not be ignored. Something a good deal like his thesis had appeared two years earlier (1911) in A. M. Simons's "Social Forces in American History" and a year earlier (1912) in Gustavus Myers's "The History of the Supreme Court," but they were Socialists and could be dismissed as such. The connection between corruption and Big Business, between political action and economic interest, had been shown in contemporary terms by Lincoln Steffens's "Shame of the Cities" and the writings of the other muckrakers: but they were, after all, muckrakers. Here was someone who was neither Socialist nor muckraker. He was American to the core, loaded with degrees, drenched in teaching. Professor J. Allen Smith had published, in 1907, a strikingly original book—"The Spirit of American Government"—which opened up many leads that Beard followed. But where Smith was suggestive, Beard was thorough and systematic. What was galling about him was that he used all the paraphernalia of scientific method, which had been considered a monopoly of smugness and the *status quo*.

There is a tradition to the effect that he had started with the intention of doing a biography of Alexander Hamilton, and while quarrying among the musty archives in the basement of the Treasury that had not been touched for a century, he saw the more dramatic possibilities that these documents and the state financial records disclosed for a study of the political role of the holders of government paper. At any rate, the research he did was a real *tour de force:* it could put to shame on the level of sheer scholarship anyone who sought to challenge it from his Olympian heights. The technical flaws that could be picked were few and unconvincing. The citations, where they were not from primary statistical sources, came from the Founding Fathers themselves.

What could you do with a man like that? You couldn't ignore him. You could only rage against his

indecency, question his patriotism, accuse him of fo-
menting class hatred—and bide your time.

The time came, four years later. Beard had been
watching the progress of the European war with enormous anxiety, alarmed at the submarine campaign,
fearful of the danger of Prussianism to the world,
making periodic statements to strengthen Wilson's
hand in dealing with Germany. Then, on October 9,
1917, the front pages ran the story of his resignation
from Columbia, immediately as a protest against the
dismissal of Professors Cattell and Dana in the patriotic hysteria that followed our entrance into the war,
but basically—as he explained in The New Republic of
December 29, 1917—as a protest against business control of university educational policy, and the "doctrinal
inquisition" of himself and others on the faculty by
the trustees. The letter to Mr. Butler that accompanied
his resignation is a classic of university history:

The University [he wrote] is really under the control of a
small and active group of trustees who have no standing in the
world of education, who are reactionary and visionless in politics, and narrow and medieval in religion. . . . As I think of
their [his colleagues'] scholarship . . . and compare them with
a few obscure and willful trustees who now . . . terrorize the
young instructors, I cannot repress my astonishment that America . . . has made the status of the professor lower than that
of the manual laborer, who, through his union, has at least some
voice in the terms and conditions of his employment.

If his book on the Constitution was his "Theory of
the Leisure Class," this was his "Higher Learning in
America." His own attitude was patriotic enough, but
in his generosity and his belief in freedom he could not
tolerate the gagging of others, and in his "Olympian

anger" he had to speak out. He had been hounded ever since the publication of his book by sometimes silly and sometimes vicious annoyances and pressures. But the climax was reached when President Butler failed to shield him from a stupid grilling by two of the trustees, Bangs and Coudert, about "teachings likely to inculcate disrespect for American institutions." The pay-off came in a Times editorial the day after his resignation was announced. It was called "Columbia's Deliverance," and was an answer at once to his resignation, his letter and his book:

Columbia . . . is better for Professor Beard's resignation. Some years ago Professor Beard published a book in which he sought to show that the founders of this Republic and the authors of its Constitution were a ring of land speculators who bestowed upon the country a body of organic law drawn up chiefly in the interest of their own pockets. It was pointed out to him at the time, with due kindness but frankly, that his book was bad, that it was a book no professor should have written, since it was grossly unscientific. . . . It was the fruit of that school of thought and teaching . . . borrowed from Germany, which denies to man . . . the capacity of noble striving . . . that seeks always as the prompting motive either the animal desire to get more to eat or the hope of filling his pockets. If this sort of teaching were allowed to go on unchecked . . . we should presently find educated American youth applying the doctrine of economic determinism to everything from the Lord's Prayer to the binomial theorem.

It had taken a long time, but American capitalism had finally published its review of Beard's book.

IV

Beard is the only American historian since Turner whose historical method has been widely recognized as taking the shape of a "theory" or a "thesis." This may be because he has always been more than a historian. He has always had one foot, and the firmer one, planted in political science: which may prove the meaninglessness of both labels, or may prove Robert Lynd's contention (in his "Knowledge for What?") that a historian is always a better historian when he is something else to start with. We see now that Beard's inquiry into the origins of the Constitution was only the first of a series of panels on the theme of the role of the economic in American culture. The second was "Economic Origins of Jeffersonian Democracy" (1915), a study of party beginnings which I hold the maturer and meatier book, one of the neglected American classics. The third was his theory (best found in "The Rise of American Civilization," 1927) of the Civil War not as a struggle over the slavery doctrine but as "the second American Revolution" of the capitalists against the planting class and, in sequel, the view of the Fourteenth Amendment as the logical outcome of the war in ensuring the iron-clad protection of capitalist enterprise by the courts.

Such doctrine, quite apart from the initial shock it gave in 1913, could not help leaving a more continuing mark on American thought. It was for many a harsh awakening from a fake American Dream. The premise even of the muckrakers had been of an original Eden, and a fall from grace—to be remedied by the atonement of reform. But Beard laid bare the basic struggle between democracy and capitalism and traced it back to the origins of the American state. Eden had never been Eden. The triumph of the oligarchs that Beard's contemporaries were witnessing was thus not contrary

to the spirit of 1789 but a logical culmination of it.
And what was true of the origins of the government
was true of later crises in its history. The slogans of
the propertied groups took on for many people a new
meaning. The Supreme Court issue was especially affected. For if it was true that the Constitution itself
was the product of class interests, it would follow
*a fortiori* that the same interests were operative in its
interpretation. Then what became of the divine right
of judges and their Lucretian place above the mortal
battle? Nor were the Socialists, despite Beard's pro-
testations, slow to draw their deductions. The book,
writes Joseph Freeman in "An American Testament,"
"was a byword among Socialist agitators who liked to
quote established intellectual authorities. . . . [It] established beyond question the Socialist contention that
the United States was a class society whose fundamental laws are class laws for the benefit of the bankers and
manufacturers as against the workers and farmers."

Beard has often disavowed this claim that his book
proved the Socialist thesis. While I think he has under-
estimated the effect of Marxism on the climate of
opinion from which he drew his doctrine, he has undoubtedly been accurate in distinguishing between
Marxist thought and his own. He has traced his own
intellectual genealogy back to Madison, Hamilton,
Webster, Calhoun and Emerson: and beyond them to
Harrington and Aristotle. There has been, he contends,
a tradition of economic emphasis in native American
political thought. This is a healthy reminder for those
who equate "economic" with "un-American." Under
the stress of the attack on him, Beard has increasingly
underlined this dissociation. And actually one may

trace in his writing a decided attenuation of the economic interpretation of history—if one starts, for
example, with his statement in his 1913 book that "until
the theory of economic determinism is tried out, it cannot be found wanting," then goes on to the explanation
in his 1935 edition that he meant merely that the
economic factor must be included among other factors
in history, and ends with his treatise on method in
history, "The Discussion of Human Affairs" (1936),
in which he concludes that the whole problem is really
very difficult and full of intangibles.

The fact is that Beard, like other social thinkers in
his tradition, has never made up his mind on the central problem of the role of the economic in history. His
book on the Constitution was the closest he came to a
formulation. In some ways it was oversharp, in others
not sharp enough. It was oversharp by making the economic interpretation a theory of men's motives rather
than of men's ideas. Spurred no doubt by a desire for
definiteness and precision which is not to be found in
the history of ideas, and by a need to protect himself
against the charge of vagueness, Beard cut out for himself too big a job—to show that the members of the
Convention stood to gain in immediate and personal
economic advantage by the outcome of their work.
This was an unnecessary *tour de force of* research. It
is as if, in seeking to explain the anti-New Deal rulings
of the Supreme Court majority during the constitutional crisis of 1935–37, one were to seek to show that
their own investments were at stake. What was relevant in a theory of economic conditioning was the relation between class and group interests on the one hand
and ideas and behavior on the other. What was rele-

vant was not the property *holdings* of the members of
the Convention but their property *attitudes*. To be sure,
their attitudes might be inferred from their holdings—
but it was a roundabout procedure and one that laid
Beard open to the charge of stressing the crass aspects
of men's motivations. His enemies made the most of it.

Here a more Marxian approach, rather than a
straight Madisonian one, would have been helpful.
For on the plane of the history of ideas, the Marxian
view stresses attitudes as outgrowths of interests: and
the attitudes of a particular individual need in no way
be related to his sense of a direct economic interest.
They may be only his borrowings from the prevalent
climate of opinion—which in turn, but at a remove,
rationalizes class interests. Had Beard taken such a
view he would have been able to solve the basic
dilemma in his book of being caught between a denial
of the disinterestedness of the Founding Fathers and
a denial of their patriotism and sense of national interest. Again and again Beard talks of the "wise" Fathers:
yet most of his readers must have been puzzled as to
how they could be selfish and "wise" at the same time
—unless one premised a sort of enlightened selfishness
such as may be found in Adam Smith's "economic
man." One answer is that many of them felt, and could
afford to feel, unselfish and patriotic: for there was no
fault line between their sense of class interest and the
prosperity of the new nation. And when that prosperity
came it ratified their wisdom, whatever their intent,
and made saints of them.

It is significant that when Beard published his sequel
on Jeffersonian democracy, no comparable cry of anguish arose from the propertied groups and their

spokesmen. He had moved away from the Fathers to the less sacred precincts of Jeffersonian politicians and theorists. And it is also significant that when Beard came to discuss the framing of the Fourteenth Amendment he should have seen in it, as Louis Boudin has recently pointed out, a "deep purpose" in the nature of a conspiracy. A theory of direct economic motivation leads quite naturally to a penchant for seeing conspiracies.

But these criticisms should not blind us to the importance and influence of the book. Its importance lay in the directness with which it cut through the whole tissue of liberal idealism and rhetoric to the economic realities in American history—and therefore in contemporary American life as well. Its influence is not to be measured by its sales, which, after the initial flurry on publication, dribbled along year after year until new interest was awakened by the New Deal constitutional crisis. Beard's book on the Constitution is one of those books that become a legend—that are more discussed than read, and are known more for their title than their analysis. But in a quarter-century its thesis has increasingly seeped into our history-writing—although a recent study shows that most of the primary and secondary-school textbooks either ignore it or mention it only for refutation. It is not hard to guess that this is because school supervisors are still fundamentalists.

# IX.

# Richards's "The Principles of Literary Criticism"

## By DAVID DAICHES

IVOR ARMSTRONG RICHARDS was born on February 26, 1893, at Sandbach, in Cheshire. He was educated at Clifton and at Magdalene College, Cambridge, where in 1915 he received a First in moral sciences. In 1922 he was appointed college lecturer in English and moral sciences; since 1926 he has been a Fellow of Magdalene College. He was visiting professor at Tsing Hua University in Peking, 1929–30; he was visiting lecturer at Harvard, 1931; and in 1936 he gave the Mary Flexner Lectures at Bryn Mawr. His recreations, he says, are travel and mountaineering.

His first two books were "The Foundations of Esthetics" (with C. K. Ogden and James Wood, 1921) and "The Meaning of Meaning" (with C. K. Ogden, 1923). The latter is regarded by many as the basic work in modern semantics, that is, the science of meaning or communication, a study that is now engaging the attention of several brilliant critics and political scientists. His collaborator in these two books, Charles Kay Ogden, born in 1889, is a little known writer who has exerted an influence out of all proportion to his reputation. Ogden has edited a whole series of scientific works on the problems of speech and communication in general, besides inventing a simplified language called Basic English.

Richards, on the other hand, has been more concerned with the problem of communication as it applies to literature, and has tried to find a psychological basis for literary judgments. His books since "The Principles of Literary Criticism" include "Science and Poetry" (1925), "Practical Criticism" (1929), "Basic Rules of Reason" (1933) and "Coleridge on Imagination" (1934).

I. A. RICHARDS published his "Principles of Literary Criticism" in 1924 as a volume in the International Library of Psychology, Philosophy and Scientific Method. Here was no woolly transcendentalism, no chatter about truth and beauty and other "universals," but an attempt to examine the nature of literary value by first formulating a psychological theory of value and then examining the processes of literary appreciation in the light of that theory.

Everybody was impressed: even the very pure esthetes were awed though not convinced. The reviews, if often hostile, were nearly always respectful. Critics pointed out the limitations of Richards's psychological theory of value, the inability of the "scientific" method to probe into the mysteries of poetry, the undue confidence with which he tackled complex problems; but they admired the author's gallant attempt to think out again from the beginning the whole business of literary criticism. Richards himself called his book "a machine for thinking with," but his critics were inclined to credit him with a more comprehensive aim. As time went on, it became generally accepted among the older critics that Richards was "important" but of course mistaken, while the younger critics, especially those who had come, directly or at second hand, under Richards's influence at Cambridge, regarded his work as the most impressive single contribution to criticism of the century and set themselves to apply this method.

To understand the contemporary reception of the "Principles" we must know something about the state of criticism at the time when the book appeared. Nineteenth-century criticism had finally disposed of the Horatian conception that the function of literature is to put a sugar coating on the moral pill and so "teach delightfully," but no generally accepted alternative theory of literary value had been produced. There was any amount of vague transcendent talk by some quite eminent thinkers, but practical criticism tended to become more and more impressionist, more and more autobiographical and descriptive. The autobiographical tendency merged into the "art for art's sake" theory at the end of the century, and criticism as a normative activity, as an attempt to assess the worth of particular works with reference to some general view of the nature and function of literature, became increasingly rare.

As a reaction against the resulting confusion, there developed in the present century a search for a positive theory of value which would dispose alike of the impressionists and the hazy transcendentalists. The cooperation of the sciences, in particular the comparatively new science of psychology, gave impetus to this search. Attacks from the scientific point of view on the assumption that poetry is a mystical activity with no definable relation to other human activities became increasingly common. At the same time an attempt to ground literary criticism in ethics—*i.e.,* to restore in

a changed and more satisfactory form the long discred-
ited Horatian view—gained rapid ground, culminating
in the "New Humanism." Thus the scientists and the
moralists were engaged, each group in its own way,
in a serious attempt to build up a positive theory of
literary value.

The "Principles" came as a contribution from the
side of science. As such it was suspect both to the ethical
critics, who agreed with its aims but disagreed violently
with its method, and to the impressionists, whom the
book attacked both directly and indirectly. These two
groups criticized the book, and made endless wisecracks about it; but they took it seriously—so seriously
that often their wisecracks sounded like attempts to
laugh off what they felt unable to disprove. In addition, Richards's ruthless application of psychological
theories in his investigation of value in human activity
aroused the opposition of most traditionalists, who
regarded the book much as contemporary theologians
regarded "The Origin of Species." The interesting
point is that both supporters and attackers agreed on
the book's importance from the beginning.

There has been no substantial change in these views
of the "Principles," except that both traditionalists and
"new humanists" have dwindled in numbers, the latter with surprising rapidity. But of recent years a new
school of critics has arisen—the Marxist or, more generally, the sociological critics. These have not chal-
lenged the importance of Richards's work, but, where
they discuss it (which is unexpectedly seldom), they
indicate that while true enough as far as it goes, it
gives a false impression because of its incompleteness,
presenting a part as the whole. The general reaction

to Richards's work is one of high respect on all sides, though only a few critics—and chiefly those with a psychological training—are willing to accept it without reservations.

## II

Before he can proceed with his positive contribution in the "Principles," Richards has to dispose of the greatest obstacle to a scientific treatment of his subject. And so he gives us a chapter on "the phantom esthetic state," where he dismisses the view held by so many romantic critics that there is a type of esthetic experience which is wholly unlike any other kind of experience and can only be described in its own terms. Literature must be put back on the map of human activity before criticism can have anything profitable to say about it, and Richards essays this important task right away. He does his job in a negative way: he proves the complete unreality of the romantic "esthetic state." As a result, literature and the other arts automatically take their place in the world of normal human experience. Anti-impressionists of various brands benefited by this clearing of the ground; in particular the Marxists owe a debt to Richards of which perhaps they are not aware.

But this dismissal of mystical absolutes is only the preliminary step in Richards's formulation of his view of literary value. He proceeds at once with his scientific attempt to base criticism on accurate *description*. Believing as he does that once critics concern themselves with describing the psychological processes that take place in both writer and reader a basis for indefinite progress has been laid, he shares the optimistic belief in progress that has been characteristic of scientists since the days of Francis Bacon. "It should be borne in mind," he says in his Preface, "that the knowledge which the men of A.D. 3000 will possess, if all goes well, may make all our esthetics, all our psychology, all our modern theory of value, look pitiful." Thus criticism is linked to those aspects of knowledge which advance with new discoveries, and the assumption is made that these discoveries will probably be constant and regular. The scientific nature of the endeavor is stressed; the aim is "to link even the commonplaces of criticism to a systematic exposition of psychology."

Psychology, then, is Richards's science. Qualities in objects are discussed not as independent facts, but in terms of their effects on persons who experience those objects. We may ask how Richards derives a theory of *value* from mere *description,* however accurate. Psychology is a descriptive and not a normative science. This problem is solved quite simply by assessing value strictly in terms of *function.* "Anything is valuable that satisfies an appetency," and the most valuable psychological state is that which involves the satisfaction of the greatest number of appetencies consistent with the least number of frustrations of other appetencies. A subtly balanced organization of impulses becomes the ideal. The first positive contribution, then, which Richards makes in his book is the formulation of this general psychological view of value—what might be termed psychological humanism.

A psychological theory of value having been arrived at, there remains the equally important task of applying it to literature. We observe functions in the human organism and arrive at a theory of value dependent on those functions: now we have to apply that theory to external objects that "act on" the organism. But what do we mean by "act on"? Can literature really "cause" states of mind? To answer these questions Richards has to turn from considerations of value to a consideration of how literature can produce value, how words can communicate attitudes which result in a valuable state in the reader.

Much of the central portion of the "Principles" is taken up with discussions of types of experience and the technique of their expression and communication. The function of the poet as the transmitter of a valuable attitude is stressed: an attitude is valuable when it represents the organization of impulses for "freedom and fullness of life." The arts in general are powerful agents in the transmission of such attitudes, which can result in permanent modifications of the mind-structure and so have lasting good effects. In this way Richards reunites art and morality through psychology.

Such an approach can offer some very interesting and helpful analyses of separate aspects of the poet's activity, both as experiencer and as transmitter, and here Richards gives us some of his most suggestive chapters. More fundamental, however, is the view of the nature and function of the poet which emerges. The two main distinguishing features of the poet are, first, that he has his past experience more readily on tap than other men have, and, second, that he is, in a special sense, a more normal person—his responses to the stimuli which constitute the formal elements of art (*e. g.,* rhythm and meter) must involve a minimum of eccentricity on his part, for it is only by having these things

in common with his readers that he can communicate
to them the new attitude, the more elaborately balanced organization of impulses, the transmission of
which is his main function and justification. The argument is developed with illustrations and examples, and
some conventional critical questions are reëxamined in
the light of Richards's theory as a whole. There follows a further elaboration of his general theory of
value as applied to the arts, which seeks to explain on
what we might call psychologico-humanist grounds why
good taste and sound criticism are not merely optional
luxuries, but an essential part of any adequate civilization. The book concludes with further discussions of
points raised earlier, of which the most persistent concerns methods of employing language and the states of
mind which give rise to these methods. We can see
that combination of interest in semantics and in logic
which has been so noticeable in recent Cambridge
thought and which is responsible for the rise of logical
positivism.

III

The influence of the "Principles" has been at least
as important on the negative as on the positive side. It
has been largely responsible for the final breakdown of
the "magical" view of literature, the view that literature, like art generally, is a mystical activity unlike any
other. And this in turn has meant the gradual elimi-
nation from serious criticism of the simple "Oh, how
wonderful" approach. On the positive side the influence
has been less uniform. In grounding a theory of value
upon description, Richards has, all unwittingly, fathered
a host of rather muddle-headed critics who seem to

have been unable to see that only a psychological concept of function can bridge the gap between the descriptive and the normative. Using some of Richards's scientific tools (with tools from the Freudians and others) but without following his scientific method, these critics have confused a description of psychological origins with an assessment of value. Thus, what Herbert Read calls a "Defense of Shelley" is simply an attempt to show that in view of his psychological make-up Shelley could not have written otherwise than he did: this, of course, tells us nothing of whether the poetry is good or bad or of what the value of poetry is. To tell us how something arose is not necessarily to say anything about its quality or subsequent function. This is a confusion—the confusion between origins and present value—that has run through a great deal of recent criticism, especially in England.

But Richards cannot be held responsible for the confusions of those who may be utilizing some of his ideas, any more than he is to blame for the host of dilettante psychologists who regularly pass off impressionistic chatter for profound analysis simply by the use of psychological terminology. Richards himself has studied with some care behaviorism and Gestalt psychology, and speaks of these matters with nothing of the amateur awkwardness that characterizes some who are called his disciples.

More desirable and more important is the influence Richards has had on serious and informed critics who are interested in the problems of literary form, poetic imagery and meaning. Here the application of psychology, encouraged by Richards, has proved most illuminating, and some of the best work done in practical criticism today, especially in America, is in this field. Psychology has not only won the right to recognition as an important tool in investigating the processes of literature, but that right is also being increasingly justified in practice. William Empson on ambiguity, George Rylands on poetic diction, the Scrutiny group (who have many individual foibles) on problems of culture generally, all seem to owe something to Richards, while in this country Kenneth Burke, among many others, has been applying psychological knowledge to discussions of poetic form. Without accepting Richards's system— his general view of value, of civilization and of the relation of the arts to other kinds of human activity— these and other critics have profited by using some of his tools effectively.

Thus the influence of the "Principles" has been threefold. First, it has helped to eliminate obscurantism from criticism. Second, it has, through no fault of Richards's, contributed to a common contemporary confusion between explanation of origin and demonstration of value. Third, it has provided new and important critical tools which have on occasions—though by no means as often as might be wished—been used with considerable skill. Richards's general philosophy has had little obvious influence on criticism. It might be added that the "Principles" has been frequently reprinted and is still, for a book of its kind, widely read; so that there is no reason to believe that its influence is at an end.

## IV

We have noted that the logic of Richards's work consists in a movement from description to evaluation, with the concept of function introduced to bridge the two. But there remains the problem of transferring a view of value in states of consciousness to a view of value in literature. For a work of literature to be valuable it must produce a valuable state of mind. *How* it can do this Richards discusses in his present chapters on meaning and communication, as well as in the earlier book that he wrote with C. K. Ogden, "The Meaning of Meaning." But *whether* any given work of literature actually does produce such a state of mind is a question that he does not fully answer.

This is one of the most serious weaknesses in the book, and it seems to arise from the fact that Richards is not nearly so well up in literature as he is in psychology. It is extraordinary that in all his discussion of literary value he never refers to more than a handful of concrete instances, and that these are all short poems. In his reaction against the view which regards qualities in art, such as Beauty, as existing wholly objectively in the given work, Richards insists that Beauty is simply the effect of the work on those who deem it beautiful, and as a result starts his inquiry by discussing states of consciousness, forgetting for the time being all about art. When he has achieved an adequate theory of value that will apply to states of consciousness, he goes back to his works of art with the cheerful assumption that his theory will apply, that adequate works of art will be those that take their origin from such states in the author and communicate them to the reader. But nowhere is there a sustained attempt to prove this. We have the feeling that literature is being forced into the pattern by somewhat Procrustean methods.

Richards maintains that literary evaluation must be

based on "a general theory of value which will show the place and function of the arts in the whole system of values." But there seems to be a confusion here in the use of the term "general." A *general* theory of value can mean either (1) a theory of value which applies not only to art but to other human activities also, or (2) a theory of value which is based on "universal" psychological factors and assumes consistent causation for these factors. Now with the first sense of the phrase we can have no quarrel: it is one of Richards's outstanding merits that he relates literary to other values. But he tends to confuse this first sense with the second, which raises much more doubtful points. The operation of the psychological factors which interest Richards is not consistent: it varies with the social context which plays so large a part in determining attitudes. Richards does consider various minor causes of variation, but only as eccentricities to be eliminated: the continual and overwhelming importance of the social factor is overlooked.

Richards's general position could perhaps be called psychological Benthamism. In Chapter VII of the "Principles" he states quite explicitly his view of enlightened self-interest in psychological terms: "It may very well be the case that a person's own interests are such that, *if he understood them,* were well organized in other words, he would be a useful and charming member of his community." It is interesting to note how closely Richards's habits of thought link him with the Utilitarians of the last century: he shares their confidence, their optimism, their individualism, their method of approach. The chief difference lies in the particular psychological theory he employs. And some of the same objections that have been brought against Utilitarianism can be brought against the views expressed in the "Principles." The whole argument tends to oversimplification. A utilitarian psychology may be relevant in the discussion of the individual *qua* individual, but in any wider context there is bound to be a conflict of utilities which cannot be resolved so cheerfully. (The individual as such is a theoretical abstraction, anyway.)

Actually, Richards's theory of adjustment of impulses is more relevant to a consideration of civilizations than of individuals. The tests he applies in his later "Practical Criticism" might be even more profitably applied—were it possible—to representatives of different civilizations. Such a test would illustrate the relativity of Richards's standards and the importance of the question of contexts. The wider our context the more relative our judgments, because terms like "adjustment" cease to be final as soon as we look beyond our self-imposed horizon, and the question "adjustment to *what?*" becomes more and more insistent. Richards is surely right in regarding literature as a means to a desirable end rather than as a desirable "thing" in itself; but there are many possible and equally desirable ends, which require integration. And further, these ends are not separate and distinct, but have complex and shifting relations to each other. The desirability of any given end cannot be gauged by contemplating it in isolation, as Richards tends to do; it can be assessed only with reference to the context within which it occurs.

The relation of art to morality, Richards maintains, has been misunderstood in the past because the whole

nature of ethics was misunderstood. Both the Horatian
pill-gilders and the Humanists failed to appreciate the
real nature of the connection between art and morals,
since their view of both art and morality was inadequate. For Richards, "the problem of morality, the
problem of how we are to obtain the greatest value
from life, becomes a problem of organization, both
in the individual life and in the adjustment of the individual lives to each other." His theory of ethics arises
directly from his psychological theory of value. But
here, too, the limitation of context harms the argument. You cannot discuss adequately questions of pattern in an indeterminate or shifting context not recognized as such. In his reaction against "abstract principles and general rules of conduct" Richards goes too
far in the other direction.

But the great importance of Richards's chapter on
art and morality lies in its pointing the way to a reunification of the two at a quite different level from
that reached by the "classical" critics. He makes that
unification himself through a reinterpretation of both
art and morality in terms of his psychological theory
of value. A moral man is the man whose coördination
of activities is the widest and most comprehensive com-
patible with the minimum of conflict, starvation and
restriction. The artist expresses and communicates such
a state. This is all very useful, if inadequate, doctrine;
obviously, we require a higher level for our synthesis
than the simple psychological one. But even if Richards's formulation here is unsatisfactory, his view that
a reinterpretation of the nature of ethics and of art is
necessary, as a preliminary to their reunification, has
proved very valuable for modern thought.

What, then, has the value of the "Principles" proved to be? It raised fundamental problems which have been setting writers to work ever since. Richards demonstrated once and for all the essential relation between literature and other forms of activity, and showed psychological knowledge to be a fundamental part of the critic's equipment. He went further, and regarded it as the only important part; but we may benefit from his discussion without accepting this extension of the argument. The points made by Richards and erected by him into a comprehensive theory of value have been separated out again by later critics, who believed Richards's system to be premature. Many valuable critical activities, such as the application of psychology to the discussion of literary form, derive from Richards's pioneer work. If the issues which Richards raised as aspects of a rather arbitrarily unified system have been split up and are being investigated one by one, as a preliminary to a more profound synthesis, that is all to the good.

# X.

# Parrington's "Main Currents in American Thought"

## By BERNARD SMITH

VERNON LOUIS PARRINGTON was born in Aurora, Illinois, on August 3, 1871, but was brought up in Kansas, where his father practised law. He attended the College of Emporia for several years, then went to Harvard, where he was admitted as a junior to the class of 1893. After being graduated he returned to Emporia to teach, remaining there five years. In 1898 he went to the University of Oklahoma as professor of English, and in 1908 went to the University of Washington, where he remained until his death on June 16, 1929.

At Washington he developed the series of courses in the history of American thought and literature from which grew his "Main Currents in American Thought." He was an extremely popular teacher, but was little known outside his own campus. Even in academic circles he was anything but celebrated—until the publication of his great work. It is remarkable how few things he published. A few reviews, a chapter in "The Cambridge History of American Literature," a monograph on the "Connecticut Wits," an essay on Sinclair Lewis, a few contributions to the Encyclopedia Britannica and the Encyclopedia of the Social Sciences—such were his publications until the appearance of his "Main Currents" in 1927.

R<small>ARELY</small> are works of literary history so widely praised as Parrington's "Main Currents in American Thought." The fact that he had written not merely history, but politics, economics and philosophy as well, makes this critical unanimity all the more remarkable; and the fact that the point of view throughout the work was radical makes it astonishing.

The applause was not limited by regional considerations. Since Parrington was a professor at the University of Washington, we would expect the Western papers to be flattering. But so were The New York World, Post and Times, The Nashville Tennesseean and The Dallas News. Nor was there a division of opinion, as there so often was in the 1920's, between journalistic and academic critics. Among the latter we would expect Dr. Henry S. Canby, then at Yale, to be cordial. But so were Professors Jay B. Hubbell, then at Southern Methodist, Samuel C. Chew of Bryn Mawr and Fred Lewis Pattee of Pennsylvania State College.

Professor Pattee, author of standard textbooks which, in some respects, were indirectly contradicted by Parrington's work, said of the latter: "It is by far the best history of American literature that has yet appeared."

Even his philosophical (or political) opponents were friendly. Professor Norman Foerster, the "Neo-Humanist," writing in The Saturday Review of Literature, took pains to announce himself antagonistic to liberalism and commented gloomily on the gloomy morality of mechanism, but admitted graciously that history written from a liberal viewpoint was better than history written from no viewpoint at all; and, on the whole, he thought well of Parrington's accomplishment. Of course the radical critics were favorable.

Institutional recognition followed: in 1928 "Main Currents" was awarded the Pulitzer Prize for History —and this was the first time a work on literature had so been honored.

The least enthusiastic of the reviewers were the two who wrote, strangely enough, for The New Republic —which proves only that strange things sometimes happen in liberal magazines. The first was Percy H. Boynton of the University of Chicago, who said many kind things about the two volumes which had just been published (spring, 1927), but described their virtues with considerable restraint. No one could object to his fault-finding, for the faults were there, but one missed in his review any feeling that he was face to face with a great work or at least a work of great significance. The second critic was Professor Morris R. Cohen of City College, who wrote on the series as a whole when the third and final volume was published in January, 1931, uncompleted because of Parrington's death two years before. Professor Cohen, who started his collegiate career as a mathematician and whose secondary vocation is lecturing on the theory of law, took Parrington to task for failing to mention the contributions to American thought of our leading scientists and legal theorists. This could be shrugged aside with a reference to Parrington's subtitle, "An Interpretation of American Literature from the Beginnings to 1920," and to the opening sentence of his Introduction to the first volume: "I have undertaken to give some account of the genesis and development in American *letters* of certain germinal ideas that have come to be reckoned traditionally American. . . ." Surely it was sufficiently generous of Parrington to have expanded the meaning of "letters" to include journalistic, political, theological and philosophical writings; to satisfy Professor Cohen he would have had to violate his declared purpose to a degree that would have nullified it. Professor Cohen's other criticism was that Parrington had neglected the more intangible esthetic values (some call it "the soul") in the belles lettres he had discussed. It so happens that the curse of American literary history had been the traditional passion for awarding artistic merits and demerits, as a result of which we had been getting a stream of dull, unenlightening and often imitative books. Mr. Cohen was scolding the one work in the field that, having broken with that tradition, had succeeded in being intensely provocative and illuminating.

The nay-sayers formed an infinitesimal minority, however, and even they were indisposed to speak solely of deficiencies. Professor Cohen, for example, used about a quarter of the space at his disposal for an appreciation of Parrington's style, vitality and "insight." . . . Why was this frankly unorthodox work so well received in so many quarters? Why did it make so deep an impression upon critics and literary historians?

II

Historiography in this country had been undergoing a thorough transformation ever since the beginning of the century. The study of economic and social forces as determining factors in the politics (and therefore the ideology) of any given period had gradually increased until it was now almost respectable as a method of analysis. By the 1920's, at any rate, the older and more reactionary historians were slowly retreating before the "vulgarians" who were not satisfied with an "inspiring" narration of events and refused to treat the affairs of parties and states as reflections of ideas which had sprung absolutely from immortal mind. Moreover, these new historians were usually progressive, in the sense that they were not blindly patriotic and were sympathetic to the struggles of the small business man, the farmer and, in some cases, the worker. The new history expressed, in brief, the rise of middle-class liberalism. Its fruits were such writers as James Harvey Robinson and Charles A. Beard.

It is fair to assume that their method was influenced, however remotely, by Marxism, although Dr. Beard quite shrewdly gave credit to James Madison. Certainly the whole movement was tied up with the advance of materialism as a consequence of a prospering scientific and industrial era. History, too, would become scientific—by being founded on measurable things: the observed environment as a conditioner of men's actions, and the concrete and practical interests which actually motivated them.

This academic revolution had barely touched the writing of literary history before Parrington. The work of Moses Coit Tyler, C. F. Richardson and Barrett Wendell had gathered moss, but their approach, "modernized" and corrected, was still being followed. Our numerous professors of American Literature had doubtless read Taine but they were apparently unimpressed when it came to using a comparable procedure in the study of their own specialty. They had, of course, never read the dialectical materialists. Several praiseworthy short histories had appeared since Wendell's time— Trent's, Cairns's, Boynton's—but their worth rested upon their scholarship and *esthetic* liberalism rather than on any fundamental difference from the older works in either method or political philosophy.

The time was overripe for Parrington's arrival. The progressive spirit had made itself felt in the books and essays of such teachers as Carl Van Doren, Robert Morss Lovett, William Ellery Leonard and T. K. Whipple, not to speak of the periodical and newspaper critics who commanded most of the non-academic public. The war and post-war generations were decidedly responsive to the attitude which those writers expressed. They were decidedly unresponsive to the tory attitude which had prevailed in our literary histories —that attitude which Dr. Canby so politely labeled "Federalist" in his salute to Parrington as a refreshing and valuable novelty. A change from the "Federalist" —in other words, Brahmin and right-wing Republican —bias was indeed due and welcome.

At the same time the materialist approach, in the form of economic determinism, was attracting notice as a way out of what Parrington called the "arid desert" of romantic philosophy on the one hand and the sterility of pure esthetics on the other. For one thing, historians like Beard, Turner, Adams and Schlesinger, by investigating economic and social problems, were revising previous notions of America's past, and their revisions made the old-fashioned textbook conception of our literature look a little silly. Furthermore, increasing interest in American writing had stimulated research in the sources: monographs on the circumstances in which the classic Americans had done their writing, doctoral theses on cultural as well as esthetic borrowings, were appearing in the journals and upsetting familiar prejudices. Van Wyck Brooks's studies, grounded on a genuine appreciation of social movements, were disturbing academic complacency. The insistence of the radical critics, the people around The Masses and The Liberator, that literature is a social product and that its history cannot otherwise be understood was also having some effect.

Dissatisfaction with the inherited way of interpreting our literature was accordingly widespread. Some of it was aimless, some of it aimed up blind alleys, but much of it was potentially fruitful. It was all formally recorded in a volume called "Reinterpretation of American Literature," which appeared in 1928 but expressed what had evidently been simmering in the colleges ever since the war.

Parrington's "Main Currents" was not the complete answer, but it went a long way toward supplying the most needed things: an account of our literary history

which squared with recent works on the history of our
people and a realistic technique for analyzing the rela-
tionship of a writer to his time and place—in addition
to a militantly progressive spirit. Professorial and
literary circles had consciously been waiting for such a
work, and if the one that did come forth was somewhat
more radical than some people cared for, it simply
couldn't be rejected. The author was a professor too;
his scholarship was sound; and his ideas were expressed
in terms that were native American, most of them having come over shortly after the "Mayflower."

### III

The three volumes form a fairly systematic history
of American literature. From the Puritan divines to
the modern realists, from the political essayists of
colonial Virginia to the disenchanted liberals of this
century, he discusses every important writer and every
literary movement this country has produced. He deals
with the esthetic achievements of the poets and the
novelists; attempts to characterize and evaluate them.
But that is a minor aspect of his work, and the least
successful. What really interested him were the social
ideas that these writers expressed. Whether he was
dealing with a poet or a political economist, it was to
the writer's basic thought about the way men ought
to live together that Parrington eventually came. He
was, as he said, *interpreting* American literature—
interpreting what it has stood for, what it has tried
to do to American life, from the point of view of
egalitarian radicalism.

I emphasize Parrington's radicalism because it is

probably the most significant aspect of his "Main Currents." A kind of environmental or sociological interpretation of literary movements had already been gaining favor. He sharpened it, gave it point, by making it definitely economic, because of his desire to reveal the motivating interests and real direction of specific works of literature. Thus his method was part of his general intention. It is inconceivable that he would have investigated with such firmness the social ties of individual writers or been so eager to expose the sectional and class issues underlying the ideological tendency which each writer represented, if his sympathies had not been lower-class. Nowadays "class-angling" is not a sport of kings.

Radical—not just liberal or progressive—is the word. He had none of that amiable tolerance which comes of cynicism, nor was he the kind of optimist whose buoyancy is based upon an Olympian idealism. He was partisan from the start—passionately so. He was optimistic because he believed, after serious economic and political study, that when the illusions of the frontier were completely dispelled and wage slavery grew openly oppressive, the people would take matters into their own hands and enforce their due rights. The third volume, with its chapters on Whitman, Henry George, Wendell Phillips and Bellamy—all of whom he embraced, yet softly, unobtrusively impugned as lacking in political acumen with regard to an industrialized, corruptly governed state—is proof enough. In the earlier volumes, dealing with figures whose words barely touch upon modern problems, his sentiments were not quite so apparent, although surely they inspired his tributes to Roger Williams, Sam Adams,

Paine, Theodore Parker and others, and his pieces on the tories for whom his scorn shone through his poised and judicious treatment of them.

His radicalism was not altogether obvious. He was certainly not so foolish as to flaunt it: he expressed his point of view as being "liberal rather than conservative, Jeffersonian rather than Federalistic"—a formulation which is not merely traditional to this country, but which has a strong appeal to large numbers of its citizens. His method he would likewise describe with classical references; in commending Beard's "An Economic Interpretation of the Constitution" he remarked: "Underlying this significant work was a philosophy of politics that set it sharply apart from preceding studies—a philosophy that unsympathetic readers were quick to attribute to Karl Marx, but that in reality derived from sources far earlier and for Americans at least far more respectable. . . . It goes back to Aristotle, it underlies the thinking of Harrington and Locke and the seventeenth-century English school, it shaped the conclusions of Madison and Hamilton and John Adams, it ran through all the discussions of the Constitutional Convention, and it reappeared in the arguments of Webster and Calhoun." Professor Eby, who edited the final volume, said that Parrington was inspired first by Taine and then by J. Allen Smith, "who applied to the abstract theorizings of political science the economic realities. . . . Parrington was quick to realize the fruitfulness of economic determinism when applied even to literature."

We cannot know whether Parrington made these "respectable" attributions because he realized that that was the only way to win a fair hearing or because, being himself wholly American in temperament and thought, they were natural to him, came to him more easily than such names as Marx and Engels. Probably both reasons operated. Nevertheless, I can state dogmatically that he had some acquaintance with Marxism, had been influenced by it, and knew that his method was related to it. I have seen a letter by him in which he said as much. Is that influence not written into the book itself? He did not speak merely of "environments" or vaguely of "economic groupings"; he did not describe a given epoch as a whole, possessing characteristics shared by all who lived in it; he spoke clearly of classes and class struggles. Essentially agrarian in mood and outlook, he was yet aware of the problems of the urban proletariat and, we suspect, convinced of the hopelessness of rural individualism and the need for socialism. This has been overlooked by those metropolitan intellectuals who were charmed by his agrarian leanings. The evidence is strewn throughout the completed parts of the third volume and is confirmed by Professor Eby's statement that Parrington had planned a vindication of Daniel DeLeon, Debs and Victor Berger.

It would be wrong to infer, however, that he was an outright socialist or a true Marxist. So far as his personal attachments were concerned, he was too much the Western libertarian to stand exclusively for collectivism. He would not repudiate the philosophical "main currents" that formed his own mind. As for the differences between his method and Marx's, some of the major shortcomings of his work arose from that earlier and so-called "American" species of materialism—shortcomings which were caused by the inadequacies of economic determinism and would not have been caused by a sound Marxist approach. For example, his brief chapter on Longfellow was an excellent characterization of the man and his writings but made no real attempt to explain the social origins of the culture from which he came and none whatever to show us the ultimate effect of his sentimentality. We must suppose that Parrington failed here simply because economic determinism is too crude and vulgar an instrument for such purposes. Another example was his lamentable chapter on Poe, where he just threw up his hands and said that Poe was "quite outside the main current of American thought" and had therefore best be left alone. In other words, economic determinism could not contribute anything toward an understanding of Poe. But a more subtle materialism—one in which cultural and psychological phenomena are integrated with the social—might have contributed something.

But there were compensations. If Parrington had been a socialist of unmistakable redness and had adopted an "alien" materialism, he would probably never have won so wide an audience or had so profound an influence. The time was ripe for him but not for a genuine Marxist. His willingness to shelve his method when confronted by esthetic problems was pleasing to literary scholars who had learned only yesterday of its applications to political controversy. That early American method enabled him to insinuate his ideas into quarters ordinarily closed to radical ideas. The thought itself was early American—in language. He spoke always of democracy, one of the noblest words we know, but one subject to various definitions. Parrington referred to economic democracy, which hasn't got an explosive sound. His devotion to that kind of democracy, which takes all other kinds for granted, and his persistence in evaluating writers in the light of it, got across. And that was his great achievement.

It was important for a weightier reason than the fact that it ended the monopoly on academic literary history previously enjoyed by conservatism, which is inherently anti-democratic. It restored the original poets, prophets and preachers whose real characters had been hidden or suppressed by the genteel school. It showed us their true faces—their antagonism to the robber barons, their love of freedom, their faith in the social decencies. Only an impassioned democrat would have brought to light those neglected features of men like Bryant and Howells or have refurbished our rusty pride in rebels like Tom Paine and Sam Adams. The job was so well done, so undeniably valid, that no one has since tried to undo it. Parrington's portraits of America's libertarians and revolutionaries are permanent, no matter how much his estimates of their minds may be corrected by the future.

He was thus in the contemporary line of critics who have been reinterpreting our heritage while searching for a "usable past." Indeed, he was the product of that self-conscious activity, the critic who did find the usable past. Since his time American radicals have followed his lead and have begun to adjust themselves to the native democratic tradition which he brought back to us and unashamedly glorified. Direct and immediate was his effect upon the writing of literary history: several recent textbooks are noticeably different from any produced ten or twenty years ago, whether because he gave the professors heart or because he taught them. It is safe to say that thanks to him a consciousness of social forces and a liberal political spirit are present in these recent volumes and to predict that they will be present in a great many more in the future.

Those are the things for which we must honor Parrington. They reduce to trivia his esthetic errors of judgment, which, by the way, are known to everyone. Who will be harmed by his fantastic overpraise of Cabell? Who will not be benefited by his insight into the nature of the American mind?

# XI.

## Lenin's "The State and Revolution"

By MAX LERNER

NIKOLAI LENIN—or in later years V. I. Lenin—was the revolutionary name adopted by Vladimir Ilyich Ulyanov. He was born on April 22, 1870, at Simbirsk, Russia, where his father was an inspector of primary schools. At an early age he was drawn into the revolutionary movement through sympathy for his older brother, who was executed after taking part in a conspiracy against Alexander III. He was graduated from the Simbirsk high school at the top of his class (1887) and entered the Law Department of the University of Kazan. Soon afterwards he was expelled for radical student activities. In a village of Kazan Province he began the study of Marx's writings, which he was to continue all his life.

In 1893 he was admitted to the St. Petersburg bar. In 1895 he was arrested as a revolutionist and imprisoned for fourteen months. In 1897 he was arrested again and sent to Siberia, where he first adopted the name "Lenin." The next twenty years were spent chiefly in exile. After the three years in Siberia (1897–1900), there were five years in western Europe, during which he edited a newspaper, Iskra, wrote incessantly, devised party policies and became head of the Bolshevik (or majority) faction of the Social Democrats, which had split away from the Mensheviks. Lenin returned to Russia to take part in the abortive revolution of 1905, but left again in 1907. During his last ten years of exile, his writings and party activities made him the leading Marxist thinker and organizer that the revolutionary working-class movement has produced.

After the Bolshevik revolution in November, 1917, he was president of the Council of People's Commissars of the USSR. In 1918 he was seriously wounded by an assassin. He broke down in 1922—as a result partly of his wound and partly of his enormous labors—and died on January 21, 1924. Lenin's works are now available in a collected edition published in New York by International Publishers.

THERE IS PROBABLY NOTHING in the history of political thought that equals in dramatic power Lenin's achievement in linking in his own life the analysis and enactment of revolution. He was one of those rare persons in whom life drives no paralyzing wedges and in whom therefore there is no gap between the idea and the act. Our psychologists call this the "integrated personality" and our educators pant for it; and in the next breath they would both dismiss whomever they found possessing it as a "fanatic." This single-mindedness of purpose is an essential condition of revolutionary success; and the interplay between action and analysis has been generalized by the Marxian tradition as "the unbroken web of theory and practice." But it was Lenin's summit achievement, topping that of every other revolutionary leader we have known, to make out of his life the enduring symbol not only of tenacity of striving but of the clear unity of thought and deed. Nor are we dealing here with a reckless extremism. The extremisms belong rather

195

with the world's Hamlets and Genghis Khans, with the paralyzed intellectual as a symbol at one pole and the extroverted world conqueror at the other. Lenin's greatness lies exactly in his resolution of these polar extremes.

Yet it is not a resolution aiming merely to untie the knots in one individual's life. If Lenin sought to resolve the tensions and dilemmas in his own life, it was in order to make of himself a sharper instrument in the social struggle. The goal was always effective action; in the interlocking of thought and deed, the end-product was the deed and not the thought. One may detect in him a mild anti-intellectualism which never fails to thrust the idea back in its place whenever it seeks to become an end. In the postscript to "The State and Revolution" he explains why the book is truncated and why the final chapter was never written as planned. It was to have been on "The Experience of the Russian Revolutions of 1905 and 1917." What interfered was the second (October) Russian Revolution. "Such interference," writes Lenin with a gentle irony, "can only be welcomed. . . . It is more pleasant and useful to go through the 'experience of revolution' than to write about it." More pleasant and useful: a whole way of life is summed up in that phrase; and in it the entire tradition of the *littérateurs* who have dallied with the revolutionary dream stands rebuked.

## II

How "The State and Revolution" came to be written contains no inconsiderable part of its meaning. In 1917 Lenin was living in Switzerland as one of a little band

of revolutionary exiles from all countries. Ten years
before, he and his wife, Krupskaya, had left Russia
because the Bolshevik Central Committee agreed that
they must not become the victims of the Tsarist repression that followed the unsuccessful revolution of
1905. They just managed to escape the death-clutch of
the terror that was grimly called at the time "Stolypin's
necktie." In a weird Uncle Tom's Cabin night they fled
across the breaking ice from the Finnish mainland to an
island where they could board an unwatched mail
steamer for Sweden. For a decade they had wandered
over the face of Europe, from Stockholm to Geneva to
Paris to Cracow and back to Geneva. It was a decade
of shattering loneliness. The strength of the Russian
workers and peasants seemed utterly broken; factional
struggles between Bolsheviks and Mensheviks within
the Russian party, and between left and right-wing
Social Democrats within the Second International splin-
tered whatever strength remained into tiny fragments.
One had to face espionage and repression from without
and treachery and inconstant purpose from within. One
lived on the edge of starvation, a jangled life of frayed
nerves and obscure strivings, most tragic because it
was severed from the proletarian Russian soil.

When the war broke out in 1914, the Social Democrats in every country voted war credits, and workers
confronted workers across the trenches. Lenin's answer
was given at the Zimmerwald and Kienthal conferences,
where he rallied the remaining anti-war socialist
leaders; it was given in his book "Imperialism"
(1915), a pitiless analysis of the internal capitalist
breakdown from which the external capitalist rivalries
sprang.

But there was a deeper answer still. The betrayal of
the Marxist tradition by its accredited spokesmen
(even Plekhanov, whom Lenin had always admired,
turned patriotic; no wound could have gone deeper)
shook Lenin to the roots of his being. An individualist
thinker might have turned to an autobiographical
search, a religious thinker to solitude. Lenin turned to
first principles. Since he had organized his life not
around a single event but around a conception of history, it was to a reëxamination of the movement of
history that he had to return in these years of crisis.

The writing of "Imperialism" had enabled him to
see the implications of the World War for the revolutionary path that was to follow it. But "Imperialism"
was a work of economic analysis. The real questions
Lenin was now concerned with—revolutionary tactic,
the seizure of power, political construction and reconstruction, state forms and their succession—were
political questions. Now there was strictly speaking no
body of political theory in the Marxian tradition—in
the sense, for example, that "Das Kapital" embodied
an economic theory and "The Communist Manifesto"
a theory of history and the class struggle. There was
only Engels's "The Origin of the Family, Private
Property and the State," full of brilliant leads lost in
a quagmire of the anthropology of the day; and there
were hints in the historical and polemical writings of
Marx himself. Lenin was to bring these suggestions together, melt them in the passionate urgency of his own
mind, pour the metal into a mold of doctrine, hammer
it into a reasoned logic of revolution.

The first stage was a set of notebooks that Lenin
called "Marxism and the State." He had evidently

begun these in a random way not long after 1907; had
pursued them in the libraries of various European
cities. After the outbreak of the war his pace increased.
Cut off from action, he sat day after day in the libraries
at Zürich and Berne, sharpening the outlines of a revolutionary theory of the state. That the revolution was
coming he had no doubt. He listened eagerly for every
rumbling from the Russian masses, who were growing
ever more discontented under the collapse of the
feudal-capitalist economy and the bureaucratic war-
machine. He knew that when the revolution came it
would be different from the 1905 revolution and different from the Paris Commune: the outward thrusts
of the objective economic development that underlay
revolution were unyielding. Yet even he did not know
how close revolution was. News did not come easily to
Switzerland through the war barricades around it.
There were anti-war demonstrations in Russia in
January, serious strikes in February. Yet as late as the
end of January, in a lecture he gave on the 1905 revolution to a group of young socialists, he said, "We of
the older generation may not live to see the decisive
battles of this coming revolution."

Lenin's wife, Krupskaya, has left us in her memoirs
an account of how Lenin first got the news that the
Tsar was overthrown:

Once, after dinner, when Ilyich was getting ready to leave
for the library, and I had finished with the dishes, Bronskey
ran in with the announcement, "Haven't you heard the news?
There is a revolution in Russia"! . . . We went to the lake,
where on the shore all the newspapers were hung up. . . .
There really was a revolution in Russia. Ilyich's mind worked
intensely. I do not remember how the rest of the day and evening passed.

Lenin's reaction was immediate. "This 'first stage of the first revolution,' bred by the war," he wrote to Kollontai, "will be neither final nor confined to Russia."

The revolution must be pushed forward. The "old European pattern" of revolutions, where mass revolt has always ended with some "constitutional" middle-class regime, had for once to be broken. There came the frantic efforts to get to Russia, wild schemes of landing in an airplane, ingenious schemes for getting through on a Swedish passport and, since he did not know the language, pretending to be a deaf mute. Finally came Martov's plan of going through Germany in exchange for interned German prisoners—a plan which was finally followed and which led to the famous "sealed train" episode and the charges of being in the pay of the German government. Ralph Fox, in his vivid biography of Lenin, has described his arrival at the Finland Station, the enthusiastic ovation of the sailors and workers, his quick perception that they were not only now more revolutionary in temper than the Provisional government but more so even than the Bolsheviks themselves reckoned. Here was history unfolding itself as he had analyzed it ever since the war broke out. The forces were there: the problem was to shape events within the mold of the forces, to shape them with a sure analytical sense of their limits. Edmund Wilson, in his projected book of essays, "To the Finland Station," is quite right in using the episode of Lenin's arrival as the symbol of the point at which "the writing and acting of history" meet.

There followed months of agitating, organizing, pamphleteering. Lenin's task was at once to instil revolutionary confidence and restrain a premature attempt at seizing power. In the July Days the demonstrations got out of his control and, after their failure, a period of extreme repression set in. The story that Lenin was in German pay and had also been a police agent was sedulously spread, and he was hunted. He had to go into hiding. He stayed in hiding for months, at first in a hayloft on a little farm near Petrograd, then in a hut made of twigs; finally the chase grew too hot to make even that safe, and Lenin crossed the Finnish border to Helsingfors, disguised as an assistant fireman on a locomotive, stoking the furnace. Just before he left Petrograd he had written a note to Kamenev:

*Entre nous.* If they get me I ask you to publish my little notebook, "Marxism and the State" (stranded in Stockholm). Bound in a blue cover. All the quotations are collected from Marx and Engels, likewise from Kautsky against Pannekoek. There is a whole series of notes and comments. Formulate it. I think you could publish it with a week's work. I think it important, for it is not only Plekhanov and Kautsky who got off the track. My conditions: all this is to be absolutely *entre nous.*

The notebook was somehow procured. Lenin worked over it during August and September while hiding in the hayloft and the twig hut and finally at Helsingfors. Especially during August and September. It is clear from Lenin's letter that he set enormous store by his book. If he was killed, it would be his legacy to the revolutionary movement. "It is not only Plekhanov and Kautsky who got off the track"—in that restrained line Lenin packed his whole bitter experience of his discussions in the Central Committee during the past months, as well as his contempt for the heresies of the Mensheviks and Social Revolutionaries. And so, between sending memoranda to his comrades on the Committee, and writing such pamphlets as "Will the Bolsheviks Be Able to Hold the State Power?" Lenin worked on what was to become "The State and Revolution." Before he could get at its final chapter, he was once more swept up in the October revolution itself. The press had such a mess of more urgent work that the book was not published until the next year. By that time Lenin was at the head of the new Soviet government. And the essay that had been begun and written as a guidebook for the revolutionary movement now took on fresh meaning as the blueprint of political construction in the Soviet state.

### III

"The State and Revolution" is outwardly an unimpressive and even a dull affair. To the superficial eye it seems only a hundred-page pamphlet, stripped of adornment, filled with the clichés of the Marxist terminology. Its method is the glossator method so common in Marxist literature—the appeal to the basic texts of the fathers, the elucidation of the texts, and the use of them to refute one's opponents. It is sometimes heavy-footed and unfailingly rasping in its polemics. Where then lies its greatness?

Only the dullard will fail to see through the outward skin the ribbed intellectual strength of the book. Lenin's greatest pamphlets have with his greatest speeches the same quality of strict economy, the same intellectual flame burning the more strongly because nothing else is permitted to obscure it. Neither did he make any pretense to originality, and he follows the method of gathering and commenting on the *loci classici* of Marx

and Engels all the more severely because he wishes to
play down his own role. He felt that his job was not to
create but to restore the Marxian theory of the state.
"The distortion of Marxism being so widespread, it is
our first task to *resuscitate* the real teachings of Marx."
Actually, however, Lenin's book is amply creative in
its elements of synthesis and reinterpretation. The
bricks for a Marxian theory of the state were available
to anyone, but no one had ever put them together. And
in the process he had to reëxamine old political forms
in the light of new economic realities, with the genius
for the modern instance that Lenin above anyone
possessed.

But the work of restoration, even in a new synthesis—while in the long run of the greatest importance
—was not Lenin's only aim. Of more immediate moment was the polemical task of refuting the Mensheviks, the Social Democrats, the Social Revolutionaries,
the waverers within his own party. And so Lenin moves
from the texts of Marx and Engels to the texts of
Kautsky and Plekhanov. It is not only that he thought
and wrote most easily in this way, and that there is a
kind of dialectic native to the Marxian mind in this
sort of confrontation and resolution of opposites; but
also, as Lenin notes, the Social Democratic writings
of the Germans had "transplanted . . . with an
accelerated tempo the immense experience of a neigh-
boring, more advanced country to the almost virgin
soil of our proletarian movement." He felt he had to
destroy the influence of these writings; hence the savage
polemical method. It is as if Lenin were seeking to light
up the doctrinal darkness with the dazzling flash of
knives.

Lenin starts with a masterly restatement of the class-domination or class-instrument theory of the state. The state is simply the special apparatus of force used by the dominant class to keep the underlying classes in subjection. By its very nature it arises out of the irreconcilability of class conflicts, and its strength must grow proportionately as the class antagonisms and the "rivalries in conquest" grow sharper. This is true of capitalist democracy as it is of every other state, except that subtler means to maintain class power are used instead of force: "A democratic republic is the best possible political shell for capitalism." The whole form of the state is determined by the class uses to which it is put. As class succeeds class, the state machinery does not adjust itself to the demands of the new class power. The whole state apparatus—police, armies, bureaucracy, judiciary—must be violently shattered by the class rising to power, which replaces it by its own state apparatus. The bourgeois classes, when they came to power, created a state apparatus, basically parliamentary and bureaucratic, for their own purposes. The proletariat will have to do the same, changing the character of the state machinery in turn in accordance with *their* objectives.

Thus far Lenin's exposition has run along the traditional Marxian lines, but his emphases are interesting. One emphasis—or rather, lack of it—is the striking neglect of the theory of the class struggle proper. Lenin states it, demonstrates it and gets over with it in a single section of his first chapter. It is simply "not true" that "the main point in the teaching of Marx is the class struggle." It "was *not* created by Marx, but by the bourgeois *before* Marx, and is, generally speaking, *acceptable* to the bourgeoisie." (How much light this throws on Charles Beard's insistence, for example, that he got his class theory not from Marx but from Madison.) "A Marxist is one who *extends* the acceptance of the class struggle to the acceptance of the *dictatorship of the proletariat.*" Which leads, accordingly, to another of Lenin's emphases: on the inevitability of the capture and destruction of the bourgeois state power by the proletariat. Engels's theory of "the withering away of the state," he insists, has been distorted. It is not the bourgeois state that withers away, but eventually the proletarian dictatorship. The bourgeois state power must be captured and dissolved.

When he comes to the question of what is to replace it, Lenin reaches the heart of his argument. The experience of the Paris Commune of 1871 becomes central. The Commune as a political form replaced parliamentary bureaucracy. It remained a *representative* institution, but ceased to be a parliamentary "talking shop." It became "a working body, executive and legislative at the same time. It is, for the first time, a genuinely democratic body; in it freedom of opinion and discussion does not degenerate into deception, for the parliamentarians must themselves work, must themselves execute their own laws, must themselves verify their results in actual life, must themselves be strictly responsible to the electorate." The Commune leveled the distance between the working class and its ruling committees; it reduced the pay of all state officials to workers' pay. And while destroying the parasitic network of centralized French bureaucracy, the Communards aimed at building up and extending the genuine national unity through a new centralism—a commune of communes. Lenin would, of course, have developed this theme further in his discussion of the soviets as the political units of the Russian revolution, had he ever written his last chapter. But he wrote enough to make it clear that the new proletarian state forms already existed in revolutionary history, and that they did not have to be spun out of the minds of theorists.

These living historical forms Lenin calls a dictatorship of the proletariat, and the whole book must be seen at once as an argument for its inevitability and a pæan to its nature. It has, according to Lenin, two principal features. On the one hand it is a *dictatorship,* in which the proletariat shares power with no other class, and in which the hypocrisies of the sharing of power are stripped away. On the other hand it is an *expansion of democracy:* "democracy for the people and not democracy for the rich folk." What seems to us a paradox—the combination of dictatorship with democracy—is to Lenin no paradox at all. Democracy for the vast majority, he argues, is possible only when accompanied by suppression of the exploiting minority through force. When the latter task has been achieved, the state machinery itself becomes useless, and increasingly withers away. The first phase of communist society—social production—gives way to the "higher" phase of a completely classless and therefore a completely stateless society. Socialism will make possible a huge technological development, which will in turn give labor a new dignity and change the whole character of consumption habits. How long a time will be necessary for this transition, Lenin insists, or what forms it will assume, it is impossible to say in advance: like all other questions of political forms, that of the withering away of the state depends on an economic base of changing institutions and habits.

IV

It would take a volume at least as long as Lenin's to discuss with any thoroughness the meaning and validity of his argument. Actually an entire literature has already developed around the book. Lenin has been used by every group in the factional struggles of the Marxists since his death. What is more pressing is for those who seek to stand outside the factions to examine what his thought means for the socialist tradition in the crisis democracies.

It is almost a quarter-century since Lenin's book was written. That quarter-century has witnessed the enactment of part of his vision and the dissolution of another part. The dictatorship of the proletariat in the Soviet Union has proved its strength and its capacity to fashion its own economic and political forms. But the world proletarian revolution, of which the Russian Revolution was to be only the beginning, has not been realized. In its place have come fascist movements, carrying the reactionary swing farther than Lenin ever foresaw. The Kornilovs, the Kolchaks, the Denikins of his own experience have become the Hitlers of ours. In this context the bourgeois democratic states present a facet which Lenin recognized but did not emphasize —that of temporary barricades against the threat of universal barbarism. The crisis of the socialist tradition revolves today around two basic and interrelated questions. First, how can fascism best be fought and a democratic socialism achieved? Second, what attitude does this imply for left-wing democratic groups toward such crisis democracies as the New Deal?

There is one line of political reasoning current today that runs directly counter to Lenin's whole position: the contention that the state is not the political instrument of any class, but a sort of broker or mediator between classes. The vivid illustration advanced in behalf of this view is the New Deal itself, which can scarcely be spoken of as an instrument of the capitalists without arousing more ironic laughter than any theory can bear. But Lenin has anticipated it with a quotation from Engels: "By way of exception . . . there are periods when the warring classes so nearly attain equilibrium that the state power, ostensibly appearing as a mediator, assumes for the moment a certain independence in relation to both." And one may add from the experience of today's crisis democracies that such a state arises only in periods of dire capitalist emergency, that it always minimizes the necessary concessions to the working class, that its hands are tied by reactionary elements within its own ranks, and that when threatened by genuine proletarian militancy it never fails to make common cause with the capitalists who hate it. I have found nowhere in the literature of political theory insights as acute as Lenin's into the ways by which democratic political forms are used to mask the fact of actual economic inequality. Maury Maverick, for example, is miles away from being a Marxian, as also is Thurman Arnold. Yet "In Blood and Ink," like "The Folklore of Capitalism," spells out in terms of the American experience the ways in which the forms and the rhetoric of our culture conceal the actual logic of oligarchy and inequality within it—less so under the New Deal but residually even there.

But if the class-domination theory remains valid as against the mediation theory, what shall we say of Lenin's insistence that the machinery of the capitalist democratic state must inevitably be captured and shattered, and that there is no path of continuity without violence between it and a democratic socialism? I do not propose to enter here into the interminable discussion whether the People's Front policy of the Comintern was a betrayal of Lenin's reasoning or was a promising but unsuccessful attempt to fulfill it under conditions he did not foresee. What interests me much more is that Lenin's own book contains two divergent lines of direction.

One of these strains is the inevitability of a violent revolution. The other is the uniqueness of each national experience, and of the economic development, the political forms and the revolutionary temper of each. The first leads to an austere anti-reformism and a bitter rejection of all Fabian assumptions. The second leads to an emphasis on the "national question," on national traditions and temper and, in Engels's words, on the theme that "the working class can only come to power under the form of the democratic republic." Can these strains be reconciled? If ever a generation will have the impulsion to reconcile them, it is one like ours, conscious through fascism of the tenacity with which the ruling class can cling to power, but conscious also of the reckless costs of violence as a method. What is healthy in Lenin's tough-mindedness is the insistence that Fabianism is never in itself a solution, since the ruling class will never in the end surrender power with-

out a desperate attempt to smash democracy itself. But
we may argue nevertheless that Fabianism and violence
do not exhaust the alternatives: that, by Lenin's own
reasoning, the fulfillment of the promise of a democratic republic leads in the deepest sense to a democratic
socialism; and that revolutions of the majority, like
the Jeffersonian, Jacksonian and the New Deal revolutions, must in the end, if conducted with courage and
skill, make an anti-democratic capitalist coup merely
suicidal adventurism.

Less immediate but no less important are the implications of Lenin's analysis of the nature and pace of
socialist development itself. Our American generation
will not accept his thesis that in a socialist state the
workers' government will share power with no other
class. What this has come to mean historically is the
one-party system and the suppression of all opposition
groups. But does this necessarily follow even from a
class-domination theory of the state? There can be no
doubt that in a minority-dominated capitalist state, the
capitalists find it possible to share their power with the
other classes. Why should this not be even more possible in an eventual majority-dominated workers' state?

This is not to deny Lenin's thesis that each new social
system must fashion its own political instruments in
terms of its own social purposes. But it is to deny that
this means a clean sweep of the political machinery of
the past. In fact, the essence of the Marxian theory of
history is that the most valid elements of one stage survive in the next. Lenin himself insists, in his chapter on
the Paris Commune, on the distinction between its dis-
carding of parliamentary forms and its retention of
representative forms. In the same way, the basic ele-

ments of the democratic tradition—the competition of ideas and of political opinions, and the democratic control of bureaucratic action—must not only be retained but expanded in a socialized culture.

In his analysis of the administrative machinery under socialism, Lenin mixes a good deal of hard sense with some curious utopianisms. He saw the need for administrative centralism if the economic machine were to run. He anticipated the *expertise* of the soviet state when he remarked, in answer to Kautsky's "superstitious reverence" for the "ministers" of the Prussian state: "Why can they not be replaced, say, by commissions of specialists working under sovereign all-powerful Soviets of Workers' and Soldiers' Deputies?" He relied, for democratic checks on the bureaucracy, on the recall of officials, the leveling down of their pay to that of the workers, and the imposition of executive responsibility on them which would force them to test their plans in practice. What seems utopian is his belief that eventually all distinctions between the officials and the population as a whole would disappear. "Under socialism, *all* will take a turn in management, and will soon become accustomed to the idea of no managers at all." Certainly that has not happened in the soviet state after two decades, nor is it likely to happen anywhere. We are more and more coming to recognize that the modern state, whether socialist or capitalist, cannot do without a bureaucracy but must learn to control it. In the beginning of socialized planning, the state technicians are bound to have a power that strains the limits of democratic safety. But in the end the problem of democratic controls must be confronted squarely.

I prefer to omit, as beyond my interest or powers, all

discussion of Lenin's theory of the transition from socialism to the "higher stage" of a classless, stateless society. Some day this may have some relevance for us. Today it remains in the realm of the luxuries of speculation. What is not in that realm is the democratic temper which pervades Lenin's whole life, and in the light of which his militant plea for dictatorship must be judged. There is no one in the history of political thought who guided himself more surely by contact with the masses, and by an amazing genius for discovering what the ordinary man thought and felt and an invincible belief in his essential dignity.

v

This book by the stocky bald little revolutionist, with its bristling militancy and its crabbed style: does it seem strange that it should have shaken our world? It has become a truism to say that the success of the Russian Revolution was unthinkable without the genius of Lenin's leadership. By the same token it was unthinkable without the confident analysis that enabled him to bludgeon the Central Committee into heeding his plans for a seizure of state power. But the converse is also true: the successful establishment of the soviet state gave the book an authenticity and a prestige that has made it one of the great twentieth-century classics.

No book that has been discussed thus far in this series has been as widely read as Lenin's. In America it sells in editions of a hundred thousand, in the Soviet Union in editions of millions. Tens of millions have read it all over the world, and their minds have beaten to the rhythm of its logic. Lenin has become the supreme symbol of the revolutionary tradition, and through that symbolism even his mannerisms and his excesses have been ratified. After Lenin, the dwarfling revolutionists without his talents nevertheless aped his withering phrases and, without his saving flexibility, they pursued his rigor.

Yet this is of trifling moment when weighed in the balance of Lenin's legacy as a whole. He wrote his book on the eve of a successful revolution: we read it today on the threshold of what may be a black period of re-action. Yet if we recall that Lenin began his researches for it in a similar period, during the years of exile after the 1905 failure, it should do much to dispel our sense of defeatism. For the long view that Lenin took is as valid in our day as in his. If we reject some of his formulations, it is because we have learned something from that history from which he himself was always learning and which he helped to shape. To the Marxist tradition he has given its most effective figure, and in the movement of Western political theory he is in his realism one of the two or three towering figures since Machiavelli.

# XII.

## Spengler's "The Decline of the West"

By LEWIS MUMFORD

OSWALD SPENGLER was born on May 29, 1880, at Blankenburg-am-Harz, Germany. He studied mathematics, philosophy and history at Munich and Berlin, published a doctoral thesis on Heraclitus, and became a school-teacher. He conceived the plan of "The Decline of the West" in 1912 and prepared a draft of the first volume before the outbreak of the World War. At this time he lived meanly in a Munich tenement, and there, writing by candlelight, he revised and completed the work. It was published in 1918 in Vienna; no German edition was published until the following year. Although it was widely acclaimed, Spengler let it go out of print in 1921 and rewrote it with due consideration for recent historical events. The revised German edition appeared in 1923, and it was this edition that was translated into English and published in the United States—the first volume in 1926, the second in 1928.

When he was successful Spengler lived in a large and lavishly decorated apartment, became an art collector and acquired a fine library, but continued to keep himself out of the limelight, making few public appearances and granting few interviews. It is known that he was favorably disposed toward Hitler; he welcomed the Nazi coup. But before his death on May 8, 1936, he earned the displeasure of the Nazis by issuing a thinly veiled denunciation of anti-semitism. A postscript to "The Decline of the West" was his "Man and Technics," published here in 1932; and his reaction to the rise of the Nazis was his volume, "The Hour of Decision" (1934).

SINCE THE TIME of the French encyclopedists, party pamphlets have dominated the thought of each age. Often these pamphlets are elaborately disguised: they are ponderous works, not leaflets, esoteric in form, not popular: they parade prophecy as science and put forward their secret wishes and hopes and aspirations as if they had no other source than the objective nature of things. While an essential part of the new doctrines, in the case of a Marx, a Pareto or a Spengler, is that ideas are incapable of directing or changing the main course of events, one can hardly doubt that these pamphlets have, paradoxically, had a potent effect upon the actions of men. If in nothing else, they have brought the diffused, scattered impulses of their generation into a sharp focus.

Perhaps the greatest of these gargantuan party pamphlets was "Das Kapital"; but in our day the turn of events has given special significance to a rival document that was written during the first World War: Oswald Spengler's "Der Untergang des Abendlandes."

The English title of this work, for some reason best known to the translator, avoids the obvious melodramatic touch of the German: *Untergang* means "downfall" or "ruin," not "decline." These volumes embody the strenuous greatness, the massive energies and the underlying crudenesses of German life, experience, thought. Spengler explored the matted world of historic events with superb intellectual courage and he unraveled more than one tangled skein. But at the same time he was so completely lacking in the gift of self-criticism that he exhibited the most naïve Junker barbarisms as if they were the pronouncements of high philosophy.

That combination of barbarism and intensive culture, which has been characteristic of Germany since the woeful disintegration of the Thirty Years' War, united in Spengler's work into an explicit ideology. Spengler had a free mind and a servile emotional attitude; he presented a formidable upright figure, with a domed bald head and a keen eye, but in the presence of authority, particularly military authority, his backbone crumpled. These contradictions threaded deeply through his entire thought.

II

Conceived before the first World War and published in 1918, before it had ended, Spengler's treatise is something more than a philosophy of history. It is first of all, from the German standpoint, a work of religious consolation. It was written, in effect, to rationalize the state in which the new German found himself. In the course of two generations, capitalism in Germany had revolutionized the material means of living. The German had acquired wealth and power and a formidable position in the world by repressing all his vital impulses except those that served directly his will-to-power. But in his heart, he was not at home in this new environment. Measured by humane standards, the relatively feeble, industrially backward, politically divided country of the Enlightenment had been a better place to live: Kant in Königsberg, Goethe and Schiller in Weimar, Mozart and Beethoven in Vienna, had put the country on a cultural level that the most expensive efforts of centralized Berlin could not surpass.

If Germany was defeated in her attempt to achieve military control of Europe, all was lost; but if Germany won, too little was gained. Nothing was left except to go on with the empty conquests of the past forty years, building railroads into Bagdad, throwing steamship lines over new trade routes, manufacturing genuine Scottish marmalade in Hamburg and, above all, giving larger scope to Junker arrogance and military prowess: the easy sack of Peking had but whetted army appetites. Thought itself had long become technicized, indeed partly militarized. Those who still felt a sentimental pull toward the older and deeper German culture, who valued the ancient spirit of a Wolfram von Eschenbach, were appalled by the battlefront bleakness of the intellectual landscape.

Drawing upon world history for consoling comparisons and precedents, Spengler found them in his theory of historic development. According to him, there are two kinds of peoples in the world: those who merely live and those who enact history. The first, if they exist before the cultural cycle begins, are mere vegetables: their life is directionless; they endure on a timeless level of pure being. If they come at the end of a cycle, they also tumble into Spengler's limbo: they are fellaheen: without ambition, without creative capacity, different from the true peasant because they clothe themselves in the worn-out garments of an old civilization, continuing its forms even though they progressively lose all its meanings.

As for the actors, they experience "Destiny": they pass from a state of culture, in which life is bound up with a common soil and a deep intuitive sense of the importance of blood and race and caste, to a state of civilization, in which their waking consciousness begins to transcend their more instinctive earlier life. In this second state, they cease to be fettered to a particular region and become, instead, cosmopolitan in extension, highly urbanized and increasingly indifferent to the vital processes that mean so much to both peasant and townsman in the earlier period. Rationalism and humanitarianism devitalize their will-to-power. Pacifism gives rise to passivism. In the phase of culture, life germinates and flourishes; in the state of civilization, the sap sinks to the roots, the stems and leaves become brittle and the whole structure of the organism becomes incapable of further growth.

### III

From the organic to the inorganic, from spring to winter, from the living to the mechanical, from the subjectively conditioned to the objectively conditioned—this, said Spengler, is the line of development for all societies.

The Western European community had had its

springtime in the tenth century. This opened the new epoch of "Faustian" culture, dedicated to the conquest of infinite space and the triumphant reduction of natural forces into mere servants of the human will. For Spengler, each culture is a unified body: it is dominated by its specific idea, which in turn is symbolized by and embodied in its architecture, its mathematics, its painting, its statecraft. The Classic idea was that of a static, spatial world, without any true sense of time; its characteristic expression was Euclidean geometry. The Faustian idea, in contrast, is a dynamic world, in which space is expressed in terms of distance, movement, time; in opposition to the post and lintel of Greek construction, it utilizes the leaping arch, and its **great** symbol is the Gothic spire.

Not merely is a culture incapable, on Spengler's analysis, of receiving the ideas or the contributions of other cultures; it cannot even understand them. All intercourse with outside cultures is an illusion; it cannot take place either in time, as historic importation, or in space, as the intermingling of different cultures like the Western European and the Chinese. One might call this theory of Spengler's the doctrine of the closed frontier. It exhibits, with curious exaggeration, the self-imposed isolation of the German, which he has interpreted alternately as a symptom of the outside world's hostility or as a token of his own superiority as a member of a chosen tribe. (That Spengler demolishes his own case by undertaking to bring out the essential inner idea of each historic culture is symptomatic of the confusion that exists everywhere in his work between his human inheritance as a Western European and his purely tribal inheritance as a German.)

In Spengler's theory of cultural development there are, however, various elements of truth. In translation from one language to another, a certain intimate residue of each culture cannot be passed on; a degree of self-sufficiency, of isolation, is important for cultural development; too easy diffusion may mean complete dissipation. Moreover, the accumulation of knowledge, inventions, scientific observations, which enriches the heritage of humanity as a whole, is only partial; though much does heap up, much is also lost. Furthermore, an underlying set of motives, a *thema,* as Dr. Henry Murray has recently called it in psychology, can be detected in such a complex mass of experience as a culture. So far Spengler's intuition was sound.

But to assume that only one *thema* accounts for all the manifestations of a culture is to ignore the existence of survivals and mutations: the first, dating back to human pre-history, make up the mass of every historic culture, while the second condition its future. Spengler's views of the relation of the "idea" to the actualities of a culture carry his convenient mysticism to the pitch of high nonsense: he actually asserts that the "idea" produces the culture—a piece of disembodied platonism that no modern man can swallow. Medieval people, for example, were not medievalists: what we call medievalism is something that we discover after the fact, as a common element in thoughts and actions that proceeded from quite different premises than a belief in the medieval idea. The latter belongs to us.

Passing from his conception of the springtime phase, Spengler pointed out that the Western European was about to enter the frigid state of winter. Poetry and art and philosophy were no longer possible; civilization meant for Spengler the deliberate abdication of the organic and vital elements, and the reign of the mechanical, the desiccated, the devitalized. The region was shriveling to a point: the world city, megalopolis. The earth itself was being plated with stone and steel and asphalt, and the individual was becoming an atom in a formless mass of humanity. To succeed in terms of civilization, one must be hard: what remained of life, if one could call it life, belonged to the engineer, the business man, the soldier. Life, in short, was to reassert itself as brutality: the sole energy left centered on destruction.

This belief in the approach of civilization's cold winter has, for reasons I shall come to shortly, fascinated many of our contemporaries. Hence it is important to realize, not so much the illegitimacy of the poetic figure itself, as the even deeper unsoundness of the grand division that Spengler makes between culture and civilization by putting them at opposite ends of his cycle. These two terms represent the spiritual and the material aspect of every society, but the fact is that one is never found without the other. The overdevelopment of fortifications and castles in the fourteenth century, for example, was as much a mechanical fact as the overdevelopment of subways is in our present order, though one belongs to a feudalism of blood and caste, and the other to finance capitalism. So again the building of new towns on rectangular plans was as much a characteristic of the earliest spring of Faustian culture as it was of the autumnal period of the nineteenth century: even that "swaggering in specious dimensions," which Spengler dates from the Alexandrine period of a culture (the Colossus of Rhodes, the twentieth-century skyscraper) is equally visible in the Italian cities of the fifteenth century.

At the other end of the scale Spengler's conclusions are just as perverse. If real poets, real artists, real philosophers exist today, people who know pity and tenderness and love, then some other alternative may be left than that of embracing the "hard" life over whose fatal approach Spengler becomes so lyric. Spengler's answer to this is so openly naïve that one almost compliments it by calling it childish: it is merely to pronounce anathema on the creative activities of our time, to find it all imitation, pastiche, inferior stuff. Needless to say these are not competent judgments, achieved by sympathetic examination of the works of art themselves; they follow from the theory, and are proved by the very doctrine they are called upon to support—that alone. The profound psychological intuitions of a Freud, the novels of a Mann, the architecture of a Frank Lloyd Wright—these things, for Spengler, must be outweighed today by the cold triumphs of technical organization. To have reasons for a contrary belief would be to undermine the two great piers that support the fragile arch of Spengler's cultural cycle: the essential separateness in space and time of culture and civilization. This duality, by the way, shows how far, despite all use of living symbols, Spengler's philosophy is from being organic.

IV

To give Spengler's philosophy in these bare outlines is to do small justice to the rich texture of his thought. But one would need a whole volume to disentangle the

keen intuitions and the profound historic discrimina-
tions that Spengler made in this work from the maze
of superstitious dogmas and rickety "facts" to which
the sound parts of his thought are joined.

Spengler wrote, as a pamphleteer must write, in a
great hurry: six years was a short time for the composition of a book of "Der Untergang's" intellectual
dimensions—and pretensions: a book begun when he
was only thirty-two. In his hurry, he was forced to piece
out his real erudition with snatches of knowledge
grabbed from encyclopedias and similar works of reference: the result is a great unevenness in the quality of
his supporting illustrations. Often his most weighty
doctrines, as in his comments on the critical importance
of mechanical time-keeping, are based on unreliable
texts; and the actual historic facts are often carelessly
used—or spurned—or hacked apart in queer shapes to
fit his particular need at the moment.

Nevertheless, as a work of historical synthesis, "The
Decline of the West" was a challenging, perhaps an
epoch-making book: its originality outweighs its many
defects. To do justice to Spengler's permanent contribution one must understand that his attempt to order
history and penetrate its processes was the very work
that Henry Adams, after formulating his abortive
phase-rule, had given up in despair. No one else had
made the attempt, on a grand scale, since Auguste
Comte, though Mr. Stuart Glennie had done some suggestive study on the periodicity of world history and
the contemporaneity of great events. The ordinary historians collected and verified facts, without venturing
to suppose that there might be any underlying rhyme
or reason in them. The notion of progress had indeed

made a deep impression upon popular consciousness, and in so far as most historians had a philosophy at all, it rested upon this formula: they assumed that the long results of time had been cumulative, in the direction of human improvement.

But the theory of inevitable improvement seduced the historian's one virtue: his sense of fact. For, in its confident optimism, it failed to account for the partial discontinuity of cultures, for the falling out of valuable elements, for the reversions from civilization to barbarism that had so often occurred, for the de-building and destruction that had made the whole line of progress so erratic, indeed so questionable.

Even when these facts were acknowledged with reference to the past, the historians glibly assumed that the growth of modern science had, by its conquest of time and space and energy, made any such break or barbarism impossible in modern civilization. Annoyed by Spengler's audacious efforts to achieve synthesis and to put the history of mankind's great cultures on a comparative basis, they resorted to the pious academic practice of pointing out the inevitable errors of fact. Shocked by his prophecies of doom, they countered with the thought that man at last was a reasonable animal, subject to the ministrations of the health officer and the policeman, beyond the reach of the business cycle, to say nothing of Spengler's more remote cultural cycle. But meanwhile fascism was spreading and the disintegration of Western culture was proceeding rapidly beneath the surface in Italy and Germany: actual history was preparing Spengler's pragmatic justification.

Moreover, Spengler's contemptuous attacks upon the methodology and philosophy of the conventional his-

torians were well directed: he properly mocked at many
points at their provincial categories of Ancient,
Medieval and Modern; he exposed the unconscious
imperialism of a history that treated the experiences of
the major portion of mankind as a mere background
for Western Europe; he demonstrated the necessity of
assuming, by an act of the imagination, a point of view
within the culture under observation, in order to understand the dynamics of events and the configurations of
the pattern of life within that culture.

In all, Spengler had much to teach the historian and
the sociologist; for them he is still worth close study.
Spengler's central doctrines, indeed, need revision and
restatement, such as Mr. Arnold Toynbee has already
attempted. Much must be thrown out completely. Yet
what remains is worthy of respect: intuitions, generalizations, formulas that are very nearly of the first
order. But, like Carlyle, Spengler worshiped the man
of action too sincerely to be content with his own role
as philosopher. Though his philosophy demonstrated
that ideas and ideologues are impotent to change actual
events, Spengler wanted to be a maker of history; by
malediction and objurgation, by shouted warnings and
hysterical appeals, he sought to impose his philosophy
upon his generation.

To get the real drift of the "Untergang," one must
read the pamphlets that are all Spengler published in
the years that followed: here the hidden aim is un-
veiled. In "Man and Technics," in "The Hour of Decision," in his "Collected Essays," Spengler divested
himself completely of the pretensions of scholarly
judgment; he beat a frenzied tattoo on the drum, at-
tempting to summon together the forces of reaction.

For Spengler was no Aristotle; he was rather the active prophet of that barbarian revolution whose name was fascism in Italy, Nazism in Germany and totalitarianism everywhere. "The Decline of the West," in its very characteristics as a work of art, was an image of the fascist states that were to be erected during the next two decades; their irrationalities, their phobias, their comical limitations were all present in that work. Spengler's anathemas against humanitarianism and liberalism and pacifism, in the very hoarse stridency in which they were uttered, set the tone for Hitler and Goebbels—if a great historian could curse like a fishwife at his opponents, why need a mere politician restrain himself? In intellectual and emotional content, Spengler's utterances exhibit the same neurotic traits that one finds in the more popular expositions of fascism.

v

Few could understand Spengler's book when it was published, except those who were already in critical possession of its irrational basis and who knew how deeply this basis was laid in German thought: in Fichte, Hegel, Wagner, Treitschke, Houston Chamberlain. Those who did understand it, however, were not unprepared to grasp the shape of things to come; in particular, they had an early insight into what has now become a sinister world problem: the pathology of the German mind.

If Veblen's exploration of "Imperial Germany" gives the best account of that mind from the outside, Spengler's book serves admirably to record its solecisms from the inside. That fact gives "The Decline of the

West" a peculiar significance for the present generation. For in this book, with its stertorous savagery and
its gleeful delight in the surrender of thought to
military necessity, the downfall of the West—or at
least the downfall of Germany—was enacted before
the eyes of the world. Modern German culture in a
sense reached its apogee in this book; and at that very
moment it sank, as it has now sunk into Hitler, into
a slough of barbarism: this was *der Untergang* in very
fact.

"Der Untergang" took possession of a defeated and
war-weary world—a world so deeply degraded by the
long brutal struggle that it was possible for the vic-
torious governments of England and France to
blockade their conquered enemies against the outside
supplies of food needed to relieve their all but universal starvation. Men had everywhere dreamed of
justice, democracy, peace. But the fruits of war were
shabby efforts to achieve "normalcy," that is, forget-
fulness. Instead of peace there was a continuation of
military efforts upon other fronts, and a solemn deter-
mination, on the part of the governing classes, to stave
off the deep economic changes—as urgent then as today—that threatened their power.

The title of Spengler's book had an even more immediate appeal than its contents, which were difficult
for even the educated to understand. For the title whis-
pered the soothing words, *downfall, doom, death.* The
post-war challenge to effective, purposive action, action
in the light of human ideals, was dissipated by
Spengler's very doctrine of "pure" action—that is,
action without rational motive or cultural content: the
work of expansion and aggrandizement as practised by

the masters of the machine. The war machine, the finance machine, the power machine—these agents followed old paths, deeply rutted. So far from urging men to depart from these ruts, Spengler proclaimed that no other course was possible: history only urged the strong to gird themselves to impose greater disasters.

For according to Spengler's cyclical diagram, the moment of Cæsarism was at hand: the feeble proletariat, unwilling to fight, sapped of its very will-to-live, could be trampled down by a barbarous soldiery. Bismarck had predicted it: a lieutenant and a squad of men could disperse the Reichstag. Relatively speaking, that is in fact what happened when Hitler and his followers stepped into offices that had not so much been won by the Nazis as abandoned by their anemic opponents, seeking to appease the barbarians' appetite for power by giving in, under punctilious legal usage, to their demands. In Italy and Germany civilized men were too tolerant of aggression, too courteous to those who hated them, too skeptical of positive evil, too much accustomed to bargains, compromises, polite shifts, to fight their enemies. Not believing in power, they refused to credit the evil intentions of those who did believe in it. In the name of democracy, the "liberals" abandoned democracy to those who had promised to leave no sign of it standing. Those who valued peace more than they valued their liberties or their culture gave way to barbarian bands that valued war. The first would not fight. The second did not have to fight. The Nazis achieved their glory easily through their opponents' inglorious retreats.

So Spengler's predictions about the immediate future

of Western civilization have proved, indeed, correct.
Though these predictions were apparently based on his
wide scanning of history, actually they were founded
upon his self-knowledge and his sense of the German
character. His telescope seems to scan the widest hori-
zons; but across the eye-piece, preventing him from
seeing even through the first lens, was pasted his own
photograph. Because Spengler respected only physical
force, he prophesied with accuracy the nature of the
post-war world and he diagnosed its typical disease—
the paralysis of will, on the part of humane men and
women, which followed by sheer reaction upon the
over-keyed energies of the war itself. But for this same
reason, Spengler failed to have a true picture of history in its totality. He had no place in his scheme of
living for the very class he represented: the priest, the
artist, the intellectual, the scientist, the maker and con-
server of ideas and ideal patterns. The work of this
class, life-bestowing, life-enhancing, Spengler con-
temptuously associated with death: the fixed, the im-
mobilized, the no-saying; and he hated their activity
precisely because it curbs the raw outbreaks of animal
passion and physical prowess that his drill-sergeant's
mind gloried in.

The truth is that Spengler feared the deep human-
ness of humanity, as he feared those domestic sentiments that work against the rule of his mythical
"carnivore." Spengler recoiled from the fact, so
obvious in history, that dehumanized power in the
long run is as pitifully weak as a powerless humanitarianism. He hated the independent power of the
mind, creating values, erecting standards, subduing
ferine passions, precisely because he knew in his heart

of hearts, for all his loud contempt, that this *was* a power: a power men obeyed. If the forces Spengler worshiped had real survival value, the culture of the Jews and the Chinese would not have remained alive through centuries, to mock ironically at the triumphs of their conquerors.

Had Spengler's philosophy been true, his polemics, to be sure, would not have been needed. But on one point Spengler was close to perceiving a fact about the nature of goodness or truth—and that is, it must have organic connections with the source of physical power, whether in the human body or in the body politic. It is not the impotent who can pride themselves on chastity, nor the weak who can take refuge in their forbearance. Spengler missed the point here, as he missed it in his definition of culture and civilization, because of his essential dualism. He forgot that the body, eviscerated of mind, was no less an ideological ghost than the mind, decapitated from the body.

## VI

The capital vice of Spengler's book was that it reinforced two elements that needed resistance rather than aid. One was the massive inertia of national states and exploiting empires, still clinging to the hope of salvaging a disordered capitalism by resorting to the automatisms of war. The other was the growing dominance of the irrational. People who had lived in a state of extreme tension for years were delighted to be told that the need for humanitarian struggle was over; those who had sought to humanize the machine, to integrate institutions more firmly with human needs and purposes, could now throw off the burden of moral action; "history" sanctioned it. In various passages Spengler had muttered darkly about the deviltry of the machine and had prophesied the "flight of the born leader from the machine," but this was offset by his more general doctrine of the approaching transformation of our whole Western society into a soulless mechanism, worked by soulless men.

But if values are unreal and if humane purposes are chimerical, something else follows: the need for rational restraint disappears. To believe what one likes; freely to substitute myth for fact and lies for truth; to recognize no other law than one's subjective fantasies; to abandon all efforts at rational intercourse and rational coöperation, with their need for common objective standards; to reject all those efforts at common well-being that the democracies of the Western World had painfully struggled toward for over a century— all these attitudes now had a historic and philosophic sanction. And many Germans, in whose intellectual composition the shadow side has occupied a large place, took over wholeheartedly this aspect of Spengler's thought; they accepted the fact that the irrational exists and must be reckoned with as a motive for espousing it—which is like accepting the existence of a fire as a reason for pouring gasoline on it instead of water.

Plainly, the inscrutable and the irrational are not discoveries of modern man; the world was inscrutable to Job, and in Plato's figure of the black horse and the white horse, the force of the irrational in human conduct was fully acknowledged, just as in the beliefs of Thrasymachus Plato exposed to daylight the dark antihuman cult of power. It remained for the Nazis to make an idol of irrational violence: they gloried in it. Spengler set the example by his very manner and method. He not merely predicted the arrival of the gangster-dictator; he provided him with intellectual weapons; he outlined his program and his goal.

When one understands the sources of Spengler's philosophy of history one should not be surprised by the turn events have taken during the past decade—nor yet by the fact that Matthew Arnold's barbarians in England, through their well engineered Munich betrayal, temporarily entered into league with Spengler's barbarians in Germany. Spengler embodied the peculiar strength and the pathetic political weakness of the German people perhaps better than any other contemporary thinker has done. When Spengler spoke of the nerveless socialists of the world-megalopolis, unwilling to defend themselves against the threatening Cæsarism, he was thinking of his own "Pappenheimer." His words accurately prophesied the débâcle of Germany; they did not in the least apply to Madrid, nor did they give an inkling into the spirit in which the Czechs would have faced terrible odds, had it not been for their outright desertion by the allies they had too faithfully trusted.

Like Hitler, Spengler ignored all those brave tendencies in German life which allied it to the world humanism of modern society: forces which, during the false dawn that followed the Locarno treaty, gave Germany undisputed leadership in creative thought in science, in architecture, in city building. Spengler accepted as "real" only those elements which emphasized the German's isolation, his apartness, his savage irrationality. And because these forces, too, cannot be confined to their frontiers, he predicted, better than more hopeful philosophers, the disastrous downward course that modern civilization is now following, at a steadily accelerating pace. Through its emotional impact, Spengler's work as a whole constitutes a morbid Saga of Barbarism. It began as a poem of defeat; it finally became an epic justification of that renunciation of the human and the rational which makes the fascists of all countries, under the leadership of Nazi Germany, the avowed enemies of the rest of the race. These are ominous days and Spengler is like a black crow, hoarsely cawing, whose prophetic wings cast a gigantic shadow over our whole landscape.

# An Afterword on the Modern Mind

THERE ARE OBVIOUS CRITICISMS to be made of this book in so far as it tries, however modestly and one-sidedly, to discuss the ideas that are changing the modern American mind.

It is limited in time. By confining itself to the twentieth century, it leaves no place for the nineteenth-century books that continue to mold our thinking, not even for the two with the deepest influence on our own generation. Both "The Communist Manifesto," published in 1848, and "The Origin of Species," published in 1859, have given birth to a whole literature based on new conceptions of human life. Marx's historical materialism—the theory that "in every historical epoch, the prevailing mode of economic production and exchange, and the social organization necessarily following from it, form the basis upon which is built up, and from which alone can be explained, the political and intellectual history of that epoch"—has given a new direction to historians and political thinkers, including many of those who regard themselves as anti-Marxists. Darwin's idea of development from lower to higher forms, and of continuity between the natural world and the human world, has transformed not only biology but also the social sciences and even philosophy; it is the intellectual background of almost all the books revalued in the foregoing chapters. Yet neither Darwin nor Marx is discussed here, except indirectly.

Moreover, the volume is limited in its contemporary subject matter. By confining itself to scholarly and speculative works, it leaves no place for works of the imagination. And people might say that even if plays and poems were omitted, novels should certainly be included in our list, on the ground that about five-sixths of American reading is fiction. To that criticism, there is a fairly simple answer. We are not concerned here with American reading habits, or with literature as such, but chiefly with the sources of our ideas. Not many of them originally came from novels, for the simple reason that it is not the novelist's job to supply them. If we had discussed books like "Ulysses" or "The Magic Mountain" or "Remembrance of Things Past" merely from the standpoint of what they contributed to contemporary thought, we should have been unfair to their authors as literary artists. That at least was the decision we reached. I might add, however, that the subject was argued back and forth, and that the novels we last thought of including were those of D. H. Lawrence— not because we considered them the most important as fiction, but because they are the best expression of an important tendency, the nostalgia for the primitive that has played a large part not only in contemporary letters but in contemporary life as well.

The volume is also limited by the political temper of its editors and their advisers. Most of these are progressives in the sense that they believe in democratic control and in the possibility of social progress. The books that changed their minds are obviously not the disillusioned books that depict human beings in the mass as cowlike animals, fit only to be deluded by mock-heroic myths and preyed upon by an "élite" of "lions" or "foxes." I am quoting three words from Pareto's "Mind and Society," which was omitted from our list by almost universal consent. But Pareto is not the only author who represents that mood and tendency. By now the Italian and German fascists, who started with almost no philosophy at all, have adopted a long line of intellectual step-parents—for example, Count Arthur de Gobineau, with his "Essay on the Inequality of Races," and Houston Stewart Chamberlain, who was Gobineau's apostle, and Richard Wagner, with his blond-beast heroes out of the Nibelungenlied, and Friedrich Nietzsche, with his pitiless supermen, and Georges Sorel, the French syndicalist who converted Mussolini to his belief in social myths and the beauties of violence, and Gaëtano Mosca, the Italian sociologist who outlined the theory of the élite that Pareto would develop in systematic detail. The house of fascist thought, as Max Lerner said, has become a death-house of all nations. Yet among the scores of fascist and pre-fascist thinkers, only Spengler is discussed in this series. A place might have been found for at least one other, and preferably for Hitler himself. By forcing us to defend the ideas that we once took for granted, he has affected us more deeply than many authors whose opinions agree with our own.

And "Mein Kampf" is not the only omission to be regretted. Among those books whose influence I have had a chance to observe, there are at least five others that might have been discussed at length. For example, there might have been a chapter on "The Golden Bough," a collection of strange beliefs and customs that ends by showing an essential similarity among primitive religions all over the world, as well as by explaining the origins of many Christian rites. It is apparently not well regarded by the present generation of American anthropologists—I note that the author, Sir James G. Frazer, is not even dignified with an article in the Encyclopedia of the Social Sciences— but it has most certainly affected us at second hand, through its influence on Continental philosophers and Anglo-American poets. . . . There might have been a chapter on "Middletown," by Robert S. Lynd and Helen Merrell Lynd. Dissatisfied with the purely statistical methods that sociologists had been following, they tried to achieve another sort of objectivity by studying a typical American community as an anthropologist might study a village in New Guinea. They were making "an experiment not only in method," as Clark Wissler said in his Foreword, "but in a new field, the social anthropology of modern life," and the field is being rapidly developed. . . . There might have been a chapter on Trotsky's "History of the Russian Revolution," a book that deeply affected many people who could not be called Trotskyites. The first of the three volumes, which is also the best, appeared in this country at the end of the Hoover administration, in those half-forgotten days when an American revolution seemed just around the corner. Thus, its

effect partly depended on its timeliness. But partly it
depended on a quality lying behind the subject and
the treatment, on a mystical fervor that led Trotsky to
depict history as God and the revolution as the judgment of his God.

Our present list includes not a single book that deals
with the nature of the physical world. The omission is
explained, and I think partly justified, by the fact that
modern men are more and more preoccupied with the
social as opposed to the physical sciences. Yet there
might have been a chapter on Whitehead's "Science
and the Modern World," which examines the preoccu-
pations of the great physicists and shows the need for
a new philosophy (though not many of us are willing
to accept, or even fully able to understand, the type
of idealism that Whitehead advocates). . . . To represent the biological sciences, there might have been a
chapter on Pavlov's "Lectures on Conditioned Reflexes," a book that shows the physical basis of what
used to be called "instinctive reactions," and how they
can be changed. It also suggests, by analogy, that most
of our thinking is associational rather than logical.
Among modern psychologists, only Freud has done as
much to change our conception of the mind itself.

I do not think that any of the authors treated in this
book should have been omitted. But instead of I. A.
Richards's "Principles of Literary Criticism," we might
have discussed "The Meaning of Meaning," the book
that he wrote with C. K. Ogden. It helped to establish
semantics as the new science of meaning or communication, and to persuade many students that it is "the
essential preliminary of all the other sciences." . . .
With these six additions and this one substitution, our

study would be less incomplete. But of course no one series could do more than suggest the different facets of the modern mind.

Among the books discussed in the twelve chapters, eight were written by Americans and four of these deal with American society. Perhaps this shows that our interests are turning toward ourselves. What a similar list would be if compiled by Englishmen or Frenchmen, or by Germans at home or in exile, I could not undertake to say. Probably most of the American books that we have treated would be dropped without argument. Quite possibly the only Americans represented would be two we have scarcely mentioned: Frederick Winslow Taylor (for his "Principles of Scientific Management") and William James. And not only would the authors be different, but also the mood and subject matter of the books included. American scholarly writing has shown a single-minded interest in amassing facts and an exaggerated distrust of theories (as compare Robert S. Lynd with Karl Mannheim, on sociology, or Franz Boas with Emile Durkheim, on primitive religions). Since Veblen died, we have not produced a social theorist of international standing, or an economic theorist to compare, let us say, with John Maynard Keynes. We have shown our talent rather in branches of learning that depend on practical knowledge of what happened and what happened next. To borrow and misuse two words from John Dewey and John B. Watson, we are instrumentalists and behaviorists. That is, we are interested in how and what rather than why—in seeing how things work and what people do rather than in final causes or ultimate goals. Moreover, we have a naturally democratic spirit that is more effectively expressed in the nature of our researches—which are likely to be concerned with ordinary people—than it is in our speeches about the glories of democracy. That our list shows both these tendencies I cannot regard as a fault or a limitation. It is part of our original plan, which was merely to discuss some books that have changed the American mind.

## II

But what do we mean when we say that our minds have changed? From what previous state have they changed, and in what direction? These are questions that cannot be objectively answered, there being no surveyors' instruments to measure the peaks and valleys of opinion. Still, we can make a rough topographical picture. By turning back to one of the nineteenth-century classics, we can use it as a fixed point from which to chart the course that our thinking has followed.

John Stuart Mill's great essay "On Liberty" was published in 1859, that is, in the same year as "The Origin of Species." Since then its influence has been felt in every country that had or hoped to have a middle-class constitutional government. Reading it today, one cannot fail to be impressed by a tone of high conviction that is seldom found in the writing of our own times. One cannot fail to admire the consistency and coherence of its arguments, or to accept its guiding principle, "That the only purpose for which power can be rightfully exercised over any member of a civilized community, against his will, is to prevent harm to others." Indeed, this plea for individual freedom has such a power of persuasion that one cannot help wondering whether harm to others might not be prevented if the officials of every autocratic government were forced, against their wills, to learn whole chapters of the book by heart. At the same time, one feels that its background is pre-Marxian and pre-Darwinian. There is a curious simplicity, not so much in its arguments or conclusions, as in its unspoken assumptions about men in society.

Let me quote four typical passages:

1. As mankind improve, the number of doctrines which are no longer disputed or doubted will be constantly on the increase: and the well-being of mankind may almost be measured by the number and gravity of the truths which have reached the point of being uncontested.

2. On any matter not self-evident, there are ninety-nine persons totally incapable of judging of it, for every one who is capable; and the capacity of the hundredth person is only comparative; for the majority of the eminent men of every past generation held many opinions now known to be erroneous, and did or approved numerous things which no one will now justify. Why is it, then, that there is on the whole a preponderance among mankind of rational opinions and rational conduct? If there really is this preponderance—which there must be unless human affairs are, and have always been, in an almost desperate state—it is owing to a quality of the human mind, the source of everything respectable in man either as an intellectual or as a moral being, namely, that his errors are corrigible. He is capable of rectifying his mistakes, by discussion and experience. Not by experience alone. There must be discussion, to show how experience is to be interpreted. Wrong opinions and practices gradually yield to fact and argument.

3. No government by a democracy or a numerous aristocracy, either in its political acts or in the opinions, qualities and tone

of mind which it fosters, ever did or could rise above mediocrity, except in so far as the sovereign Many have let themselves be guided (which in their best times they have always done) by the counsels and influence of a more highly gifted and instructed One or Few.

4. In the case of any person whose judgment is really deserving of confidence, how has it become so? Because he has kept his mind open to criticism of his opinions and conduct. Because it has been his practice to listen to all that could be said against him; to profit by as much of it as was just, and expound to himself, and upon occasion to others, the fallacy of what was fallacious. Because he has felt, that the only way in which a human being can make some approach to knowing the whole of a subject, is by hearing what can be said about it by persons of every variety of opinion, and studying all modes in which it can be looked at by every character of mind. No wise man ever acquired his wisdom in any mode but this; nor is it in the nature of human intellect to become wise in any other manner.

In these four passages there is a whole series of assumptions that have since been questioned. There is, first of all, the assumption that progress is the normal state of affairs, "that the tendency of things, on the whole, is toward improvement." In other books, and notably in "Representative Government," Mill insists that he does not regard progress as automatic and axiomatic. "We ought not to forget," he says, "that there is an incessant and ever-flowing current of human affairs toward the worse, consisting of all the follies, all the vices, all the negligences, indolences and supinenesses of mankind; which is only controlled, and kept from sweeping all before it, by the exertions which some persons constantly, and others by fits, put forth in the direction of good and worthy objects." But having thus admitted the possibility of regression, he returns time and again to the idea of improvement, as if it were a law of the social universe. Indeed, for a man born in 1806, who had seen the world transformed during his own lifetime by an unparalleled series of inventions, who had watched the slow triumph of political reforms and social proprieties (with the Regency buck giving way to the philanthropic merchant), who had succeeded in his own profession while his class and country grew more powerful year by year, as a result, so it seemed, of their growth in knowledge and virtue—for such a man it was hard not to believe that the age of Victoria was immeasurably superior to the past, when the majority of eminent men "held many opinions now known to be erroneous, and did or approved numerous things which no one will now justify." And it was hard not to believe that the same process of improvement would continue indefinitely, unless it happened to be checked by restrictions on freedom of thought and action.

But freedom of thought came first. For a second assumption was that progress depended wholly on the intellect, and resulted from the "preponderance among mankind of rational opinions and rational conduct." There was of course a theoretical distinction between opinions and conduct, or wisdom and goodness, but in practice it could be disregarded, since the second almost always resulted from the first. Goodness was profitable, and men eventually did the profitable thing (after observing and discussing their mistakes, that is, correcting them by the normal processes of reason). While working toward their interests as individuals, they were also working toward the interests of society as a whole.

That leads to a third assumption, namely, that

progress was due entirely to individuals. Society was not so much an organism as the arithmetical sum of its members. In the same way, the knowledge possessed by society was a sum obtained by adding together millions of separate knowledges. That sum was being increased, as individuals discovered new truths and engaged in more diversified activities. Society as a whole was moving forward, but not as a result of collective efforts. Indeed, the collectivity had little to contribute; the best it could offer to individuals was security and freedom to continue their studies. A foolish society might prevent progress—as the Chinese had done—by requiring all men to think and act alike. But not even the wisest society could in itself achieve progress, which came about naturally through the work of "the gifted and instructed One or Few."

A fourth and last assumption concerned the nature of knowledge. Mill believed that those with sufficient aptitude might develop it by cultivating the virtues of humility and open-mindedness. The superior few, of whom he often spoke, were never instinctive or impulsive or intuitive; they never jumped to conclusions. Instead they went about improving themselves and others by looking at all sides of a case, by listening to all the arguments and comparing them, by rejecting the false and accepting the true—"No wise man ever acquired his wisdom in any way but this."

To readers of our own time, it seems that Mill wrote his great essay on a false or at least an oversimplified notion of the mechanics of social change, of the part played in it by the intellect, of the relation between the individual and society, of the nature of knowledge and the methods by which it is normally acquired. It

seems to us, moreover, that behind all his other assumptions lay the picture of an idealized creature that
might be called the Reasoning Man. This was not the
same as the Economic Man often mentioned in college
courses, since all living persons are economic in the
sense of being consumers, if not always producers,
whereas Mill believed that only one out of a hundred
was even comparatively rational. Yet this hundredth
person was responsible for the whole of human knowledge and human progress. He was a creature outside of
history as we know it; he had no acquired prejudices,
no family or class or national loyalties; he was never
ruled by animal instincts or sexual neuroses; he performed no reflexive or purely habitual actions. Except
for his bondage to reason, he was free. Indeed, he was
almost a God, almost the Unmoved Mover of medieval
theology, since he contributed everything to society at
large while receiving almost nothing in return.

The Reasoning Man was of course an abstraction,
yet Mill seems to have believed that such a creature
existed in the world about him. He believed, moreover, that this being, this entity, was strong enough to
drive barbarism backwards, step by step, using no
weapon but the pure force of its reason. He believed
that he was himself a Reasoning Man and was writing
for an audience composed of other Reasoning Men.
He believed in his own impartiality and independence,
never stopping to think that much of what he said
revealed *unconscious* motivations (the word is of our
own day), or was the result of previous *conditioning*,
or represented the *attitudes* and *frame of reference*
proper to his own *class* of highly trained administra-
tors selected from the British bourgeoisie. In those days

the bourgeoisie was triumphant, could see no end to its rule, so reason too was triumphant, and progress, always peaceful, stretched out into the future like the two safe rails of the trunk line from Manchester to London.

## III

The history of thought for the last eighty years might be centered round the attack on the Reasoning Man. That attack was a slow and complicated process, and could be described in its details only by someone familiar with all the scientific and historical problems involved in it. Still, with the passage of time, its general outlines are becoming reasonably easy to grasp.

One might say that it began by accident. After the middle of the nineteenth century, an army of students scattered into the separate sciences, almost like bees leaving the hive at daybreak in search of honey. It was a period of busy researches in all fields, but especially in those having to do with the present and past of the human species. Darwin had inspired a host of followers. There were important discoveries in biology and paleontology, in anthropology and archeology, in animal and human ecology, in the psychology of animals, children and the insane, in economic and cultural history, in social and political behavior. Each line of research was followed quite independently. There were, it is true, some efforts to smuggle ideas from one scientific field into another. Sociologists in particular would try to apply physical or biological principles to their own problems, without realizing that when the first law of thermodynamics or the theory of natural selection is torn from its proper context, it becomes merely a metaphor, and often a misleading metaphor. But in general each scientific worker applied himself to his own half-acre of his own field, finding and cultivating and labeling facts like rare flowers in a botanical garden.

The process of dispersion into specialized fields reached its height in the years preceding the World War. In those same years people began to complain of it. Observing the contrast between the order existing in the separate sciences and the utter confusion in the world outside, they called on the scientists for principles that would serve them as guides through chaos. The scientists at first resisted the call. As citizens they held their own opinions, like everybody else, and were sometimes only too eager to proclaim them; but as scientists they had no moral or political theories to offer, except an unquestioning faith in the scientific method. Part of their strength, they believed, lay in their detachment from practical life. Part of their method consisted in postponing conclusions while piling up facts and yet more facts.

But the time came when conclusions could no longer be evaded. And the time also came when even the newer sciences began to be systematized and simplified, began to grope toward broader principles that could guide researches in many fields, began to arrange themselves into a general pattern of scientific thought. In the years just after the War, "outlines" and "stories" of knowledge became vastly popular. Besides the importance for the lay public of books like "The Outline of History" and "Mathematics for the Millions," they indicated that a new development was taking place inside the scientific world. The process of dispersion was finally giving way to a process of concentration. At nightfall, one might say, the bees were returning to the hive with the honey they had gathered.

And now a curious phenomenon was revealed. The scientists and scholars who contributed to modern thought were most of them radicals in their own special fields but conservatives everywhere else. Sigmund Freud, for example, retained the social and political opinions of a mildly liberal Viennese physician while revolutionizing our picture of the human mind. Henry Adams obeyed the standards of American moneyed society while believing that those standards made it impossible for any talented man to lead a satisfactory life. William Graham Sumner began as an Episcopal clergyman, and remained a hard-money man to the end of his days, while making studies of primitive customs that helped to weaken the foundations of Christian ethics and classical economy. And so with the other men whose work is discussed in this volume. Turner, Dewey, Boas and Parrington were professors at a time when American university faculties were circumscribed by rules of conduct almost as rigid as those of a monastic order. Beard, after resigning from Columbia, became the respected first citizen of a little Connecticut town. Spengler was a German schoolmaster; I. A. Richards is a Cambridge don. Lenin, the arch-revolutionist, was conventional in his artistic judgments and his everyday habits. Only Veblen carried his rebellion into many fields, and the price he paid was neglect and lack of opportunity to pursue his studies. Perhaps that casts a light on the course that most of these authors followed. Some were conservative by instinct, but others must have made a deliberate choice. In order to avoid fruitless battles with the public, they decided to be conformists in every field except their own. And yet, when the results of their studies were fitted together into a unified pattern, the conformity and conservatism disappeared. It became evident that these deacons and professors, these bondholders and leading citizens, had collaborated in a radically new conception of human life.

One result of their efforts was the utter destruction of the Reasoning Man. John Stuart Mill had portrayed him as possessing certain attributes: he was rational, he was civilized, he was morally free, he was an individual. Now, one by one, these attributes had been stripped away from him. He was not rational; on the contrary, most of his actions were conditioned reflexes and many of them were the acting out in symbolic forms of suppressed desires; his psychology could best be understood by studying that of animals or children. He was not civilized; on the contrary, his social behavior was full of concealed survivals from barbarism and was capable of reverting at the least excuse to forthright savagery. He was not morally free, except within a limited sphere; on the contrary, he was subject to his biological nature, to his physical environment, to his class loyalties, to a whole series of laws the existence of which had not even been suspected in the early nineteenth century. And finally he was not even an individual, in the sense that Mill had used the word, since his life as a human being was inseparable from his social life. Unless he belonged to a community, he was deprived of his human heritage, he was a beast among beasts.

In other words, the Reasoning Man was exactly as

real as Milton's angels. . . . Years ago when I studied
zoölogy, my professor used to say that he did not
know whether angels existed, but in any case they had
six limbs—counting their wings—and therefore could
not be mammals. In the same fashion we might say
of the Reasoning Man that if he does exist, in some
corner of the world, his qualities are different from
those of the living men around us; he does not belong
to the human species.

### IV

At another time, people might have refused to accept
the unflattering picture of themselves that was drawn
by the newer sciences. But its accuracy was apparently
confirmed during the World War, when even our intellectual leaders showed an utter lack of reason and when
ordinary citizens behaved like savages or children. In
those years it began to be felt that modern civilization,
instead of being solidly built, was a flimsy bridge over
gulfs of barbarism. It began to be felt that progress, for
an imperfect race like ours, was difficult at best and
likely to be halted for centuries. It began to be felt that
we were approaching the end of an era, and perhaps of
our culture as a whole.

One effect of this mood, in the intellectual world, was
a tendency toward a type of pessimism that claimed to
be founded on modern science. The tendency can be
found in many authors, but it was most systematically
expressed by Joseph Wood Krutch, in his book "The
Modern Temper." Briefly, Mr. Krutch complains that
science has destroyed our life-giving illusions, including our belief in the friendliness and bounty of Nature,
with the result that "man is left more and more alone

256 Books That Changed Our Minds

in a universe to which he is completely alien." Our
sense of human dignity has also been destroyed; and
with it we have "lost the faith in life which is requisite
for the building of a Chartres or the carving of a
Venus de Milo." There is no salvation left for us in
love, or in literature, or in metaphysics, and today we
are disillusioned even with science, "not because we
have lost faith in the truth of its findings, but because
we have lost faith in the power of those findings
to help us generally as we once hoped they might help."
We might as well admit to ourselves "that living is
merely a physiological process with only a physiological
meaning and that it is most satisfactorily conducted by
creatures who never feel the need to attempt to give it
any other."

All this leads Mr. Krutch to a prophecy concerning
the fate of European civilization, a prophecy that is
particularly interesting in view of what has happened
during the ten years since his book was published. He
has been arguing that the qualities most prized by civilized men—refinement, sensitivity, skepticism, dispas-
sionate thinking—are really anti-social because they
develop the individual at the expense of the race.
Eventually, he says, these qualities will lead to the
decadence of any culture in which they flourish. Our
own culture is a case in point; it is probably decaying
already and its ultimate collapse is certain. But that,
he adds, is not the end of the story:

If modern civilization is decadent then perhaps it will be re-
juvenated, but not by the philosophers whose subtlest thoughts
are only symptoms of the disease which they are endeavoring to
combat. If the future belongs to anybody it belongs to those to
whom it has always belonged, to those, that is to say, too absorbed

in living to feel the need for thought, and they will come, as the barbarians have always come, absorbed in the processes of life for their own sake, eating without asking if it is worth while to eat, begetting children without asking why they should beget them, and conquering without asking for what purpose they conquer.

Once this picture of the future had been accepted by any large number of people—and Mr. Krutch was neither the first nor the last to present it—a new development was likely to take place. Some men would decide not to perish with the declining culture. In order to survive, they would transform themselves into the new barbarians. They would abuse and ridicule the intellect, glorify instinct and the pure act, and become so absorbed in living that they would no longer feel the need for thought. Men such as these would no longer value knowledge for its own sake, but merely as a tool, so that the immediate justification for social science would be that it taught methods of deluding the masses; for psychology, that it made good soldiers; for chemistry, that it produced new explosives with which to defeat the enemy. The final purpose they would find in all studies and all activities would be power for themselves, illimitable and unreasoning.

And that is exactly what has happened during the last ten years. Of course this process of thinking does not explain the rise of fascism, which had its real sources outside the realm of ideas. But it does explain the conversion to fascism of some few intellectuals, and the weak resistance to fascism on the part of others who had everything to lose by it. The scientific questioning of authoritarian systems of ethics would be used as an excuse for denying all ethical principles, except loyalty to the tribal leader. The scientific attack on the Reasoning Man would be used to justify Mussolini's attack on Abyssinia and Hitler's attacks on Czecho-Slovakia and Poland.

v

In the meantime the scientists and scholars have pursued their researches without being much affected by fascism, except in so far as they have been silenced by it in Germany and, in the western countries, have reacted violently against it. In truth their aims are completely opposite to those of the fascist leaders. When they explored the subconscious mind, or the physical nature of thought, or the need for myth and ritual, they had no intention of glorifying instinct and habit and faith at the expense of the intelligence. When they cast doubt on various ethical systems they were not implying that people should kill and rob to make themselves or their tribes more powerful. When they destroyed the conception of the Reasoning Man, they were not attacking reason itself. On the contrary, they were extending the domain of reason into areas where instinct and habit and blind faith had once been the only guides. In a sense, they were even enlarging the concept of human freedom. Claude Bernard, who wrote the best definition of the experimental method, said that this method is the one "that proclaims the liberty of spirit and thought." And Pavlov told his translator, Dr. W. Horsley Gantt, "Real freedom will come in proportion to our knowledge of the physiology of the brain, and we shall obtain a victory then over our own natures, as we have done over exterior nature, through scientific knowledge."

As for scientific pessimism, as represented by books like "The Modern Temper," it is largely based on a misreading of the effects of science on men's opinion of themselves. Of course it is true that the scientists have destroyed some of our cherished illusions, beginning with the Ptolemaic picture of the universe. But they have by no means destroyed the foundations of human dignity. Why is it necessary to that dignity for man to be pictured as specially created by God, in God's own image, and inhabiting the exact center of the cosmos, with the seven planets revolving about him and the stars fixed in the sky as signs that God remembered him through the night? Dignity is a social and individual quality that depends on no particular cosmology. Granting that we need a sanction for the race of man, we can find a sounder base for it in history than in theology or metaphysics. When we reflect that the human species developed after millions of years of slow evolution; that it was helpless compared with the great beasts among which it lived; that step by step it invented tools and weapons, subjugated the animals, refined its methods of communicating and preserving ideas and embarked on the conquest of knowledge and power; that it is engaged in an agelong effort, ending for each generation in tragedy but always renewed by the next, to control its physical and social environment and its own destiny; that there is no danger of its ever achieving Utopia, or more than a perilously brief satisfaction —then there is reason enough for human pride and human faith.

That, I think, is a view of mankind justified by the researches of the last eighty years. It is important to note that their effects have not been purely destructive of human ideals. Even the attack on the Reasoning Man was not so much an essay in destruction as the effort to advance another conception, that of man as a living organism in a changing society. Around this conception has been gathered a whole group of studies; indeed the tendency of modern thinking (as Kenneth Burke said in a letter that I quoted in the Foreword) has been to construct a synthesis based on the social sciences, just as the early nineteenth century constructed one that was based on metaphysics, and the middle ages one that was based on theology. All that is lacking for such a synthesis is a great systematic thinker, a Kant or a Thomas Aquinas of our own time.

I had thought to use this final article to discuss some further tendencies of modern thought—for example its preoccupation with time, and with processes as opposed to stable situations, and its emphasis on the need for carrying ideas into action, and finally its search for a historical or sociological basis for religion. But this is not the moment for such a discussion. These last lines are being written between radio bulletins of fighting on the western front and of hourly bombing raids on Warsaw. In many countries, books have been closed for the duration of the war. The doors of the libraries have been barricaded with sandbags; the laboratory windows are dark in the autumn evenings, like all the other windows.

The scientists themselves have not much comfort to offer. Like everyone else they fear that we are not so much at the beginning of a war resembling the others, as midway in a cycle of wars that could end only with a peace of exhaustion, like the peace which descended on Germany after the Thirty Years' War—that is the optimistic view—or on the Roman Empire before its final collapse, after the ceaseless and senseless battles of the third century. They realize that there is no guarantee against the collapse of our own civilization— what will its name be in the textbooks of the thirtieth century?—nor even against the self-destruction of men as a species; overdeveloped in their organs of combativeness and tools of combat they may disappear from earth, like the saber-toothed tigers. Yet the scientists have not lost hope. As long as their nations are at peace—and even afterwards, in the intervals snatched from war work—they continue to labor in different fashions at their one obsessing problem. "In the last analysis," Claude Bernard wrote in 1865, "all the sciences reason in the same fashion and aim at the same goal. All wish to achieve an understanding of the law of phenomena, so as to gain the ability to foresee, modify or master those phenomena." Today the struggle is centered in the oldest study and newest science of all, the science of history. The aim is still to gain the ability to foresee, modify or master its phe-nomena, that is, to substitute the human intelligence for blind chance or blind passions in the conduct of society. If that aim can be even partly achieved, there will be no danger that the human race will die by its own hand.

M. C.

**THE END**

# Appendix

# RECOMMENDED BOOKS

Adams, Brooks: Law of Civilization and Decay. 1895.
  Theory of Social Revolution. 1913.
Adams, Henry: The Education of Henry Adams. Privately
  printed 1906; published 1918.
  Mont-Saint-Michel and Chartres. Privately printed 1904;
  published 1913.
Adler, Felix: An Ethical Philosophy of Life. 1918.
Babbitt, Irving: The New Laokoon. 1910.
  Rousseau and Romanticism. 1919.
Beard, Charles A.: An Economic Interpretation of the Constitu-
  tion of the United States. 1913.
Beard, Charles A. and Mary R.: The Rise of American Civi-
  lization. 1927.
Bergson, Henri Louis: Creative Evolution. First in French
  1907; in English 1911.
Berle, A. A. and Means, Gardiner C.: The Modern Corpora-
  tion and Private Property. 1932.
Boas, Franz: The Mind of Primitive Man. 1911.
Boudin, Louis: Government by Judiciary. 1932.
Bourne, Randolph S.: Untimely Papers. 1919.
Brandeis, Louis D.: Other People's Money. 1914.
Bridgman, P. W.: The Logic of Modern Physics. 1927.
Brooks, Van Wyck: The Ordeal of Mark Twain. 1920.
  Three Essays on America (including America's Coming-
  of-Age, 1915; and Letters and Leadership, 1918). 1934.
Bukharin, Nikolai: Historical Materialism. First in Russian
  1921; in English 1925.

Clapham, J. H.: An Economic History of Modern Britain. 1926.

Commons, John R. and Associates: History of Labour in the United States. 1918.

Corey, Lewis: The Decline of American Capitalism. 1934.

Croce, Benedetto: Aesthetic as Science of Expression and General Linguistic. First in Italian 1902; in English 1922.

History: Its Theory and Practice. First in Italian 1919; in English 1921.

Croly, Herbert: The Promise of American Life. 1909.

Dewey, John: Essays in Experimental Logic. 1916.

Experience and Nature. 1925.

Human Nature and Conduct. 1930.

Reconstruction in Philosophy. 1920.

Studies in Logical Theory. 1903.

Dreiser, Theodore: A Book About Myself. 1922.

Durkheim, Emile: The Elementary Forms of the Religious Life. First in French 1912; in English 1915.

Eddington, Sir Arthur Stanley: The Nature of the Physical World. 1928.

Einstein, Albert: Relativity; The Special and General Theory. 1920.

Eliot, T. S.: The Sacred Wood. 1920.

Ellis, Havelock: Studies in the Psychology of Sex. 1900–09.

Fite, Warner: Moral Philosophy. 1925.

Frank, Waldo: Our America. 1919.

Frazer, Sir James G.: The Golden Bough. 1911–27.

Freeman, Joseph: An American Testament. 1936.

Freud, Sigmund: A General Introduction to Psychoanalysis. First in German 1917; in English 1920.

The Interpretation of Dreams. First in German 1900; in English 1913.

Geddes, Sir Patrick and Thomson, Sir John A.: Life: Outlines of General Biology. 1931.

Gissing, George R.: The Private Papers of Henry Ryecroft. 1903.

Gray, John C.: The Nature and Sources of the Law. 1911.

Halévy, Elie: A History of the English People. First in French 1912; in English 1924.

Hammond, J. L. and Barbara: The Town Laborer. 1917.

Hartshorne, Charles and Weiss, Paul, Editors: Collected Papers of Charles Sanders Peirce. 1931–5.

Hilferding, Rudolf: Das Finanzkapital. 1910.

Hitler, Adolf: Mein Kampf. First in German 1925; complete in English 1939.

Hobson, J. A.: Imperialism. 1902.

Work and Wealth. 1914.

Hogben, Lancelot: Mathematics for the Million. 1937.

Holmes, Oliver Wendell: Collected Legal Papers. 1920.

Howard, Ebenezer: Garden Cities of Tomorrow. 1902.

Huxley, Leonard, Editor: Life and Letters of Thomas Henry Huxley. 1900.

James, Henry, Editor: The Letters of William James. 1920.

James, William: Pragmatism. 1907.

Varities of Religious Experience. 1902.

Keynes, John Maynard: The Economic Consequences of the Peace. 1920.

Kohler, Wolfgang: Gestalt Psychology. 1929.

Kropotkin, P. A.: The Conquest of Bread. First in French 1888; in English 1906.

Fields, Factories and Workshops. 1899.

Krutch, Joseph Wood: The Modern Temper. 1929.

La Follette, Robert M.: La Follette's Autobiography. 1913.

Laski, Harold J.: Authority in the Modern State. 1919.

Lenin, V. I.: Imperialism. First in Russian 1917; in English (authorized) 1933.

State and Revolution. First in Russian 1917; in English (authorized) 1932.

Lippmann, Walter: Drift and Mastery. 1914.

A Preface to Politics. 1913.

Public Opinion. 1922.

Lipson, Ephraim: The Economic History of England. 1929–31.

Lynd, Robert S. and Helen M.: Middletown. 1929.

Mannheim, Karl: Ideology and Utopia.

Mathiez, Albert: The French Revolution. First in French 1922–7; in English 1928.

Mehring, Franz: Karl Marx. First in German 1919; in English 1935.

Mencken, H. L.: The American Language. 1919.
>    Prejudices. 1919–27.
Michel, Robert: The Sociology of Political Parties. 1914.
Mitchell, Wesley C.: The Backward Art of Spending Money.
>    1937.
>    Business Cycles. 1927.
Myers, Gustavus L.: History of the Great American Fortunes.
>    1911.
Ogden, C. K. and Richards, I. A.: The Meaning of Meaning.
>    1923.
Pareto, Vilfredo: Mind and Society. First in Italian 1916; in
>    English 1935.
Parrington, Vernon L.: Main Currents in American Thought.
>    1927–31.
Pavlov, Ivan: Lectures on the Conditioned Reflex. 1928.
Planck, Max: The Philosophy of Physics. 1936.
Poincaré, Henri: Science and Hypothesis. First in French 1903;
>    in English 1905.
Reed, John: Ten Days That Shook the World. 1919.
Richards, I. A.: The Principles of Literary Criticism. 1924.
Robinson, James Harvey: The Mind in the Making. 1921.
Rostovtzeff, M. I.: The Social and Economic History of the
>    Roman Empire. 1926.
Russell, Bertrand: Our Knowledge of the External World.
>    1915.
>    The Principles of Mathematics. 1903.
>    Proposed Roads to Freedom. 1919.
Santayana, George: The Life of Reason. 1906.
Seligman, E. A. R., Editor: The Encyclopedia of the Social
>    Sciences. 1930–5.
Shaw, George Bernard: Prefaces. Collected into one volume
>    1934.
Sinclair, Upton: The Brass Check. 1919.
>    The Goose Step. 1923.
Sombart, Werner: Der Moderne Kapitalismus. 1902.
Sorel, Georges: Reflections on Violence. First in French 1908;
>    in English 1912.
Spengler, Oswald: The Decline of the West. First in German
>    1918; in English 1926.

# CONTRIBUTORS TO THIS VOLUME

CLARENCE E. AYRES is professor of economics at the University of Texas. Earlier he had been professor of the principles of education at Ohio State University, associate professor of philosophy at Amherst and an editor of The New Republic. He is the author of "Science—the False Messiah," "The Problem of Economic Order" and other works.

CHARLES A. BEARD is identified in the biographical note preceding the chapter on "An Economic Interpretation of the Constitution."

JOHN CHAMBERLAIN is the author of "Farewell to Reform." He was formerly staff book reviewer of The New York Times and associate editor of The Saturday Review of Literature. For several years he has been one of the editors of Fortune. His reviews and articles appear in The New Republic, Harper's and other periodicals.

MALCOLM COWLEY, literary editor of The New Republic, is the author of "Blue Juniata," a book of poems, and "Exile's Return," a history of the "lost generation."

DAVID DAICHES is an Englishman, formerly a Fellow of Balliol College, Oxford, now a lecturer in English at the University of Chicago. He is the author of "Literature and Society" and "The Novel and the Modern World."

LOUIS KRONENBERGER has contributed essays and reviews to The Saturday Review of Literature, The Nation, The New York Times Book Review, The New Republic and other periodicals. He is the editor of "An Anthology of Light Verse" and of "An Eighteenth Century Miscellany." Formerly on the staff of Fortune, he is now dramatic critic of Time.

MAX LERNER is professor of political science at Williams College. He was formerly managing editor of the Encyclopedia of the Social Sciences, director of the Consumers' Division of the National Emergency Council and editor of The Nation. He is the author of "It Is Later Than You Think" and of "Ideas Are Weapons."

LEWIS MUMFORD is the author of "The Golden Day," "The Brown Decades," "Technics and Civilization," "The Culture of Cities" and other works in literary criticism, cultural history and social philosophy.

PAUL RADIN is the author of "Primitive Religion," "The Racial Myth" and other works. He has taught

anthropology at the University of California, Fisk
University and the University of Chicago, and has
held fellowships in this field from Columbia, Yale and
Harvard. He has worked for museums in Berlin,
Prague, Florence and London.

BERNARD SMITH is the author of "Forces in American
Criticism." He has contributed essays and reviews to
The New Republic, The Saturday Review of Literature, The New York Herald Tribune Books and other
periodicals. Since 1929 he has been on the staff of
Alfred A. Knopf, Inc., as an editor and in other
capacities.

GEORGE SOULE is an editor of The New Republic,
director-at-large of the National Bureau of Economic
Research and vice-chairman of the National Economic
and Social Planning Association. He has lectured at
the Yale Law School. He is the author of "A Planned
Society," "The Coming American Revolution," "The
Future of Liberty" and other works.

REXFORD GUY TUGWELL was Under Secretary of the
United States Department of Agriculture from 1934
to 1937. In the latter year he resigned from his professorship in economics at Columbia University. He is
now chairman of the New York City Planning Com-
mission and is engaged in private industry. He is the
author of "The Industrial Discipline," "The Battle
for Democracy" and other works.

# Index

277

# 278 Index

# Index 279